# JERUSALEM
## CITY OF KINGS

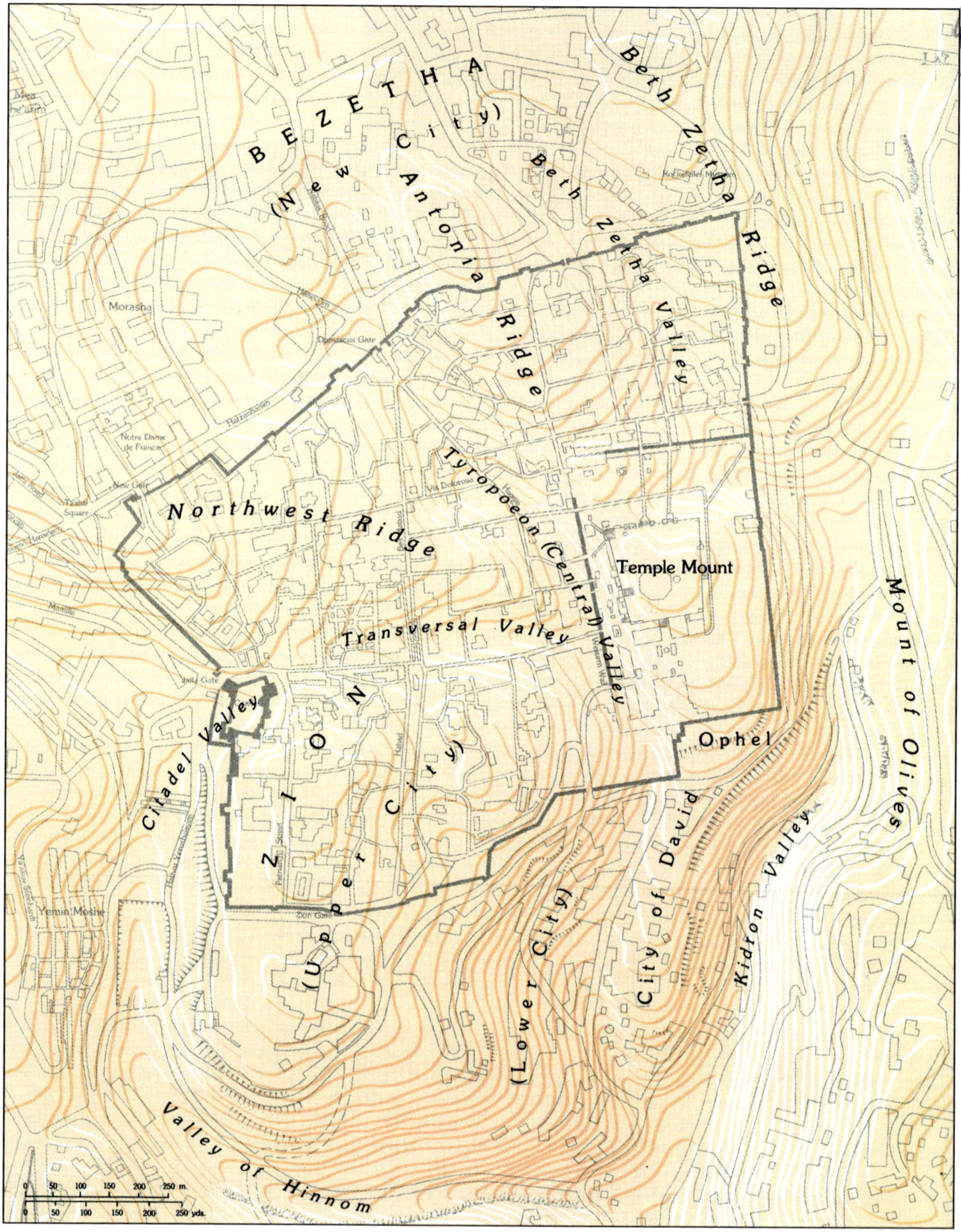


*The Topography of Jerusalem.*

Dan Bahat

# JERUSALEM CITY OF KINGS

## *A CARTA ATLAS*

Carta, Jerusalem

# Contents



# Picture Sources

8 Ophel ostracon. Courtesy of Israel Antiquities Authority.
9 Warren's Shaft (reconstruction). Courtesy of S. Cohen.
10 Siloam Inscription. Courtesy of Museum of Archaeology, Istanbul.
11 "David's Palace." Courtesy of E. Mazar.
11 Terraced structure. Courtesy of Z. Radovan
12 Entrance to Tell Ta'yinat temple (reconstruction). Courtesy of L. Ritmeyer.
12 Window frame (reconstruction). Courtesy of L. Ritmeyer.
13 Iron arrowheads. Courtesy of N. Avigad.
14 Siloam Tunnel. Courtesy of Ir David Foundation.
16 Tomb inscriptions. After N. Avigad, *Eretz Israel*, vol. 3, Jerusalem, 1954, pl. 3, 4.
16 Tomb of "Pharaoh's Daughter" (reconstruction). Courtesy of L. Ritmeyer.
17 Burial caves (reconstruction). Courtesy of L. Ritmeyer.
19 Tombs T1 and T2 (reconstruction). Courtesy of S. Cohen.
23 The "First Wall" (reconstruction). Courtesy of L. Ritmeyer.
24 Council Building (reconstruction). Courtesy of L. Ritmeyer.
26 Hasmonean period Citadel (reconstruction). Courtesy of L. Ritmeyer.
30 Palatial Mansion (plan). Courtesy of L. Ritmeyer.
32 Palatial Mansion (reconstruction). Courtesy of L. Ritmeyer.
34 Temple Mount in Second Temple period (reconstruction). Courtesy of L. Ritmeyer.
38 Entrance ban inscription. After *Quarterly of the Department of Antiquities in Palestine* VI, 1938, p. 2.
38 Stone of the Trumpeting Place (reconstruction). Courtesy of L. Ritmeyer.
39 Southwest corner of Temple Mount (reconstruction). Courtesy of L. Ritmeyer.
40 Barclay's Gate. Courtesy of L. Ritmeyer.
41 Theodotus inscription. Courtesy of Israel Antiquities Authority.
43 Herodian Citadel (reconstruction). Courtesy of L. Ritmeyer.
45 Double Gate (reconstruction). Courtesy of L. Ritmeyer.
46 Siloam Pool (reconstruction). Courtesy of L. Ritmeyer
50 Burial tomb (reconstruction). Courtesy of L. Ritmeyer.
53 Tombs of Zechariah and Hezir's Priestly Family (cross section). Courtesy of L. Ritmeyer.
54 Incised menorah design (with reconstruction). After N. Avigad, *Discovering Jerusalem*, Jerusalem 1983, fig. 154.
55 Judaea Capta coin. Courtesy of Reuben and Edith Hecht Museum, University of Haifa.
58 Map of Jerusalem as center of the world. From H. Bünting, *Itinerarium sacrae scripturae*, 1581, frontispiece.
61 Sheep's Pools (reconstruction). Courtesy of L. Ritmeyer.
62 Mounting stone. From C. Warren and C. R. Conder, *The Survey of Western Palestine, Jerusalem*, London, 1889, p. 334.
62 Jesus' tomb (reconstruction). After L. H. Vincent and F. M. Abel, *Jérusalem Nouvelle*, Paris, 1914, vol. II, fig. 53.

All other illustrations or photographs are from the picture archives of Carta, Ltd., and the author.
Due credit has been given to the artists who provided important drawings and reconstructions for the first edition of this atlas. For the current publication, some archaeological drawings have been amended by the author to accord with the latest discoveries and research. It is the author's hope that the artistic integrity of the original has been retained.
Great care has been taken to establish sources of illustrations. If inadvertently we failed to do so, due credit will be given in the next edition.

---

Translation: Shlomo Ketko; Ada Yardeni

Excerpted from Dan Bahat's
*The Illustrated Atlas of Jerusalem* © 1989, 1990, 1996
*The Carta Jerusalem Atlas* © 2011


Formerly: *The Atlas of Biblical Jerusalem*

Designed and produced by Carta, Jerusalem



Printed in Israel
ISBN 978-965-220-793-7

# Foreword

It is my hope that this *Atlas of Biblical Jerusalem*, excerpted from *The Illustrated Atlas of Jerusalem*, will be helpful to readers of the Scriptures and all those who wish to visualize the Holy City as it was in biblical times.

Jerusalem was at its apex of glory and beauty during the last century before the destruction of the Temple in 70 CE. Herod had built many magnificent edifices in the city, with the Temple and its Mount the crowning glory. These works gained fame, and the Talmud goes out of its way to describe the physical qualities of the city, which "took nine measures of beauty out of the ten with which the world was bestowed, leaving one measure to the rest of the world."

The first scholarly study of the Holy City, not surprisingly, was made by a clergyman, the reverend Edward Robinson, in 1838. His main focus was on the reconstruction of the city in the time of Jesus.

Christian sources, in describing Jesus' deeds, supply us with much information about the city. The New Testament, often the only source for the holy sites, has enabled scholars to find many of their locations in the present-day city.

Christian scholars focused mainly on the days of Jesus. Our knowledge, therefore, of first-century Jerusalem by far exceeds that of other periods. Most significant to pilgrims are the holy sites in the city and how they evolved.

The early Christian community was concentrated on Mount Zion, and there the first church was built. For the other holy sites, we rely mainly on the church fathers, whose accounts were made after the destruction of the Temple. There is a gap from the second to fourth centuries, between the events described in the New Testament and the descriptions of the church fathers, in which no archaeological or literary evidence has yet been found.

Even so, archaeological discoveries of the early churches show that their sites had already been venerated in ancient times. The traditions are often borne out by archaeological proof. Sites such as the Pool of Siloam and the Pool of Bethesda, where churches from the fifth century were uncovered, attest to the long tradition of the holy sites. These discoveries and the literary sources provide the basis for the reconstruction of the Holy City as Jesus knew it.

My thanks to the archaeologists, who gave me permission to publish the results of their latest excavations, and to the staff of Carta.

Dan Bahat
Jerusalem, 1994

**Note to the Second Edition:**
Since *The Atlas of Biblical Jerusalem* was first published in 1994, a great many excavations have been carried out in Jerusalem, mainly in the City of David. These excavations have enriched us with a treasure of new information.

Much of the results from these excavations and attendant research has been incorporated in this atlas, *Jerusalem City of Kings*, excerpted from the third updated and expanded edition of *The Carta Jerusalem Atlas*. Many thanks to my friends Eilat Mazar, Ronny Reich and Eli Shukron who shared with me the fruit of their labor and allowed me to present it to the reader.

D.B.
Jerusalem, 2012

**Note on biblical citations:**
In quoting the Bible, we intentionally used the King James Version, completed in the days of William Shakespeare. Its archaic language is in harmony with the Hebrew Bible both in majesty and simplicity. Of the King James Version, one is tempted to speculate that had the Bible originally been in English, this is the way it would have been written.

# The First Temple Period

## 1000 BCE – 586 BCE

The First Temple period begins with the conquest of Jebus (Jerusalem) by David. The description of this conquest appears in the Bible in two versions: in the Second Book of Samuel (5:6–9) and in the First Book of Chronicles (11:4–7). It would appear that these descriptions are contradictory, since in the first, David is described as actually conquering the city, while Chronicles ascribes the conquest to Joab son of Zeruiah. As the biblical text in the Second Book of Samuel is to a certain extent distorted as a result of various traditions that have merged, it is difficult to determine with any amount of accuracy whether this is a contradictory description or a different account.

The biblical account of the manner in which the city was captured is also enigmatic. At first it was believed that David conquered the city by a ruse: by entering by way of a "gutter" (according to 2 Samuel). According to this version, the city was penetrated by way of the city's water system, today called Warren's Shaft, but through recent studies, it became apparent that the shaft was built in a later period, probably at the end of the reign of King Solomon, or of one of the early kings of his dynasty. The Hebrew term *tzinor*, mentioned twice in the Bible, probably has two meanings: in our case (2 Sam. 5:8), a utensil similar to a pitchfork, used as a magic instrument with which to fend off the enemy and prevent him from conquering the city. This definition is based on the fact that the Jebusite king also used magic and placed the blind and lame on the walls, as a warning that anyone attempting to conquer the city would suffer the same fate. The second meaning of *tzinor* is a musical instrument. According to this definition, the conquest of the city was carried out in a manner similar to that of the capture of Jericho. Jericho was taken with the aid of shofars and the Jebusite city with trumpets. Support for this theory is to be found in Psalms (42:7) where the term *tzinor* is also mentioned with what would appear to be a reference to a musical instrument which gives forth a blaring sound. Menachem ben Saruk, a tenth-century Jewish sage, also explained this term as meaning a "musical instrument."

After the conquest, the royal palace called "Zion's Citadel" was renamed the "City of David." The area of the city remained the same and its boundaries were its ancient walls. The assumption that David expanded the city toward the north, in the direction of the Temple Mount, has not been substantiated. Buildings were added during David's reign, but were constructed within its original confines. According to the Bible, at first David fortified the city: "And David built round about from Millo (probably a system of terraces, which enabled construction on the steep slopes of the city) and inward" (2 Sam. 5:9) and later also built the king's palace: "And Hiram . . . sent messengers . . . and they built David an house" (2 Sam. 5:11). It would seem that the Jebusite fortress, the "stronghold of Zion," where David took refuge after the conquest of the city, was situated in the northeastern corner of the ancient City of David. This was also the site of David's palace. An artificial "tell" was discovered here, created by a system of terraces filled with stones, enclosed in box-like shapes placed one above the other. The estimated size of this structure is 39×66 feet (12×20 meters), but it could have been higher and broader. From the archaeological excavations it transpires that it was David who built these terraces, which acted as additional support for further fillings to solidify and cover over the ancient structure. Fifty-five such terraces were uncovered in excavations between 1978 and 1984. In the excavations of 1992, more terraces were discovered above the ones already excavated, and the stone debris covering them indicate that the camp was on even higher ground. It can be assumed that it was upon this tell surrounded by terraces that David extended his palace, with the assistance of the builders sent by Hiram, king of Tyre, but the top section of the structure has not survived. Kathleen Kenyon's excavations revealed architectural remains which

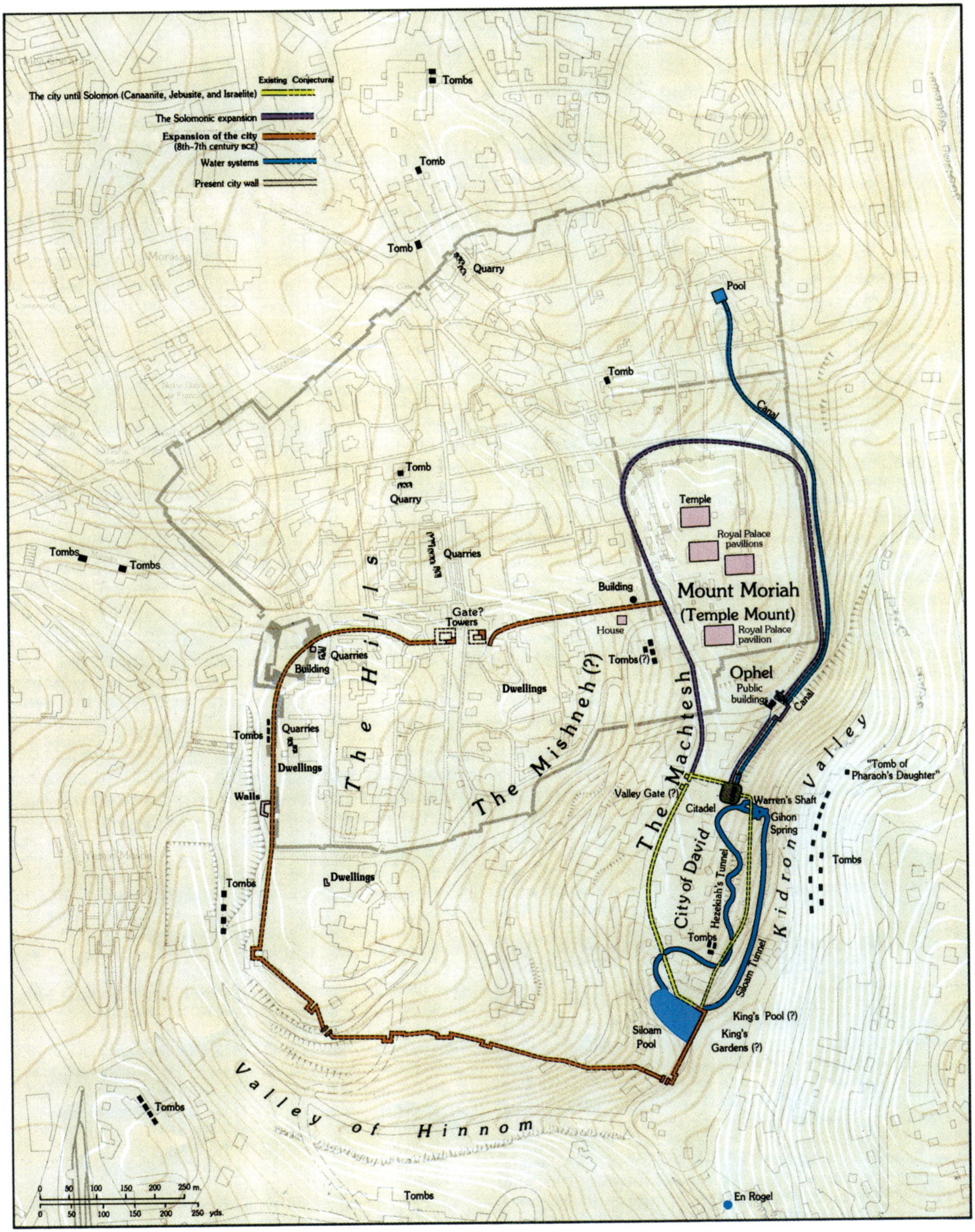

Existing Conjectural
The city until Solomon (Canaanite, Jebusite, and Israelite)
The Solomonic expansion
Expansion of the city (8th–7th century BCE)
Water systems
Present city wall
Tombs
Tomb
Tomb
Quarry
Pool
Tomb
Canal
Tomb
Quarry
Temple
Royal Palace pavilions
Quarries
Tombs
Tombs
Building
Mount Moriah (Temple Mount)
Gate? Towers
House
Royal Palace pavilion
Quarries
Building
Tombs(?)
The Hills
Dwellings
The Mishneh (?)
Ophel
Public buildings
Canal
Tombs
Quarries
Dwellings
The Machtesh
Kidron Valley
"Tomb of Pharaoh's Daughter"
Walls
Valley Gate (?)
Citadel
Warren's Shaft
Gihon Spring
City of David
Hezekiah's Tunnel
Tombs
Dwellings
Tombs
Tombs
Siloam Tunnel
Siloam Pool
King's Pool (?)
King's Gardens (?)
Valley of Hinnom
Tombs
Tombs
En Rogel
0 50 100 150 200 250 m.
0 50 100 150 200 250 yds.

could well have been those of an edifice such as a palace. These included such items as a proto-Ionic capital similar to that found in neighboring countries dating to the same period. The discovery of this tremendous building project from the time of David enables us to follow the development of the government center in Jerusalem. At first David built a palace and an administrative center on this site—a "house for David" (2 Sam. 5:11)—and once the new center was built by Solomon on the Temple Mount, the old palace began to deteriorate.

The "House of David" is not mentioned again in the sources, and private dwellings were built on the terraces. There is a theory that the tremendous terraced structure is the biblical Ophel, but we are of the opinion that the term "Ophel" refers to a high feature, such as a steep slope to which one ascends, implying the sharp peak above the area at the north of David's city, beyond the southern wall of the Temple Mount. In 2005, near the terraced structure, a public building was discovered, the largest and most important one found thus far on the City of David hill. According to the excavator Eilat Mazar, it dates from the eleventh to tenth centuries BCE. The Second Book of Samuel (5:9) relates that "David dwelt in the fort, and called it the city of David." The finds of the newly discovered building could fit the biblical description since the large stone terraced structure connected to it is in the form of a rampart, surrounding the public building as a defense. Of David it was said that he built the Millo (literally, "fill"); the network of terraces enabled extensive building on the steep slopes of the city. Later it is told that Hiram, the king of Tyre, sent building materials and builders to build "a house for David", but it is unclear if the recent discovery was indeed for "the City of David."

Solomon built the Temple and the royal palace beside it, north of the structure built by his father David. It can be assumed that this complex, described in detail in the First Book of Kings, was fortified when the city expanded northward and the Temple Mount was added to it. In her excavations of the City of David (area P), Kathleen Kenyon uncovered a section of a possible casemate wall, of the type used by Solomon to fortify several of his cities. It is possible that this section of the wall is part of the system of fortifications Solomon built while expanding the city northward in order to enclose the newly built Temple. But this is not certain, and in fact hardly any remains of these fortifications have been found. One of the reasons for this is the building that took place in this area after the First Temple period, especially under Herod, which left no trace of the buildings from Solomonic times. The fortifications depicted on the map are not based on archaeological finds, but rather on the topography of the Temple Mount. This makes it possible to determine accurately the situation of the line of fortifications, since the Temple Mount is surrounded by valleys and seasonal riverbeds. A further allusion to the fortifications of this period may possibly be found in the deep moat discovered on the northwestern side of the Temple Mount. This moat was undoubtedly dug prior to the Herodian era, opposite the hill upon which the Antonia fortress stood in Herod's time. Since there is no further evidence of other government-sponsored building on this section of the mountain, it would seem that the digging of the moat was in fact carried out during the First Temple period, or even during the reign of Solomon. If this is so, the area

*The* **Ophel Ostracon (Clay Tablet)**, *from the eighth to seventh centuries* BCE, *with the longest inscription found in Jerusalem in cursive script, was discovered in 1924 by J. G. Duncan in excavations on the hill of the City of David. The inscription was written with a scribe's pen on a whitewashed pottery sherd, but has not been preserved in its entirety and thus its exact interpretation is questionable.*

*The accepted reading of the inscription is "Hezekiah son of Karah son of Sharash son of Bakihu, Ahihu son of Hasharak son of Amakihu, Yahu son of Kari son of Amakihu." Many other readings, however, have also been suggested.*

*One of the most ancient water-supply systems in Jerusalem discovered in 1867 is* **Warren's Shaft**, *named after its discoverer, Sir Charles Warren. The shaft was apparently dug in its final stages during the First Temple period (its origins date from the Middle Bronze Age II) in order to enable the city's inhabitants, who were living inside the defense walls, to reach the spring situated outside the walls, without exposing themselves to the enemy forces in times of siege. Similar water-supply systems were found at Hazor, Gezer, Megiddo, Gibeon, and other sites, but this seems to be the most complex. It is difficult to recreate the manner in which the shaft was constructed, but the cross-section illustration will help to do this.*

*The vaulted chamber is the starting point for a visit to Warren's Shaft. This chamber was probably shaped differently during the First Temple period, and there may have been a section of a tunnel by which the hill, or rather the city itself, was reached. The present chamber was built in the Second Temple period to facilitate entrance to the shaft, and a vaulted tunnel was constructed to enable easy access and exit (today the tunnel is used for exiting only). At the bottom of the chamber can be seen the spot where an attempt was made to dig down to reach the water source, but for some unknown reason the work was stopped and another tunnel built instead. The tunnel begins at stepped levels, and its continuation is almost horizontal. This was done so as to make it possible to reach a particular point and then sink a vertical shaft to the spring's water level (the experimental shaft was put out of use and is now filled with soil). Above the shaft was a natural opening, a sort of cave, which was perhaps used by the workers as a source of light, or as a place in which to pile up the waste extracted during the quarrying. However, it serves no purpose within the water system. Until recently there was a supposition that this natural opening had a function during the course of the construction of the system. It was believed that when the attempt to dig the experimental shaft failed, the inhabitants of the city discovered the natural cave, sunk the vertical shaft from there, and only when the lower section was completed was the upper section of the system constructed. The purpose of all this was supposedly to guarantee the safety of the workers. However, this supposition has no substantiation.*

*Some two centuries after the shaft was sunk, when Hezekiah began his monumental water-supply system, he made use of the tunnel connecting the shaft and the spring, thus saving himself the necessity of quarrying in the vicinity of the spring, and enabling him to begin digging his tunnel at that spot. It was only in Hezekiah's reign that Warren's Shaft fell into disuse. However, the discovery of the vaulted chamber and the determination of the date have given rise to a new problem relating to the use of this water-supply system in the Second Temple period as well, since Josephus did not mention the spring and named the "Siloam Spring" as the water source of Hezekiah's tunnel. It appears that the entire water system, including that of Hezekiah, was not in use until the Middle Ages, and only then was the water from the Gihon Spring brought into use once more. Steps were built from the bed of the Kidron Valley leading to the guardhouse erected above.*

*The drawing does not show the recent discoveries at the site which comprise fortifications for the spring and other installations.*

occupied by the Temple Mount during his times is highly probable and well defined.

One should bear in mind that, according to the Book of Chronicles, the Temple was built on Mount Moriah, a name that was used for the mount until a relatively late date. Micah (3:12) was the first to mention the term *Har ha-Bayit* ("mountain of the house"). This name became so common that it was repeated by Jeremiah (26:18), and the Hebrew term is used to this day.

A most impressive gate (designated on the map as the Valley Gate) and discovered by Crowfoot and Fitzgerald in 1927, was considered as having been built during the reign of Solomon. However, this is not certain, and for archaeological technical reasons it could also be dated to the Hasmonean period.

The same applies to the water system, called Warren's Shaft, which was built on the hill of the City of David, to enable water to be drawn from the Gihon Spring at times of siege. There is no conclusive proof available of the date this structure was built. However, its similarity to buildings serving the same purpose in other cities, such as Hazor and Megiddo, makes it possible to surmise that it was built at the end of Solomon's reign, or under one of the kings who succeeded him. Recent archaeological excavations held in the area of Warren's Shaft date this project to the early Judean Monarchy.

The large terraced structure, which protected the royal palace during David's reign, began to deteriorate and lose importance after the administrative center of the city was moved to the Temple Mount area, where Solomon's new royal complex, including his palace and temple, were built. In the ninth century BCE, as the population increased and the large rock-hewn pool from the eighteenth century BCE fell into disuse, the pool was filled in and settled. The fill was partially

*The* **Siloam Inscription**, *from the time of King Hezekiah (about 700 BCE), was discovered in 1880 not far from the southern entrance to the tunnel. Hezekiah excavated the tunnel in order to make provision for the supply of water to Jerusalem from the Gihon Spring, which was outside the city walls, to the Siloam Pool inside the city. After Hezekiah built a new wall which brought the Siloam Pool within the confines of the city, guaranteeing the flow of water from the spnng to the city was of the utmost importance, especially in times of siege. Hezekiah's building projects are described in the Second Book of Kings (20:20) and in the Second Book of Chronicles (32:30).*

*This inscription, which is in the Museum of Ancient Near Eastern Antiquities in Istanbul, is the longest ever found belonging to Jerusalem's biblical period. It is believed to describe the meeting between the two teams of workers excavating the tunnel, and their concern over the possibility of missing each other when they were about to break through at mid-point. Following is the text of the inscription "[. . . when] (the tunnel) was driven through. And this was the way in which it was cut through: While [. . .] (were) still [. . .] axe(s), each man toward his fellow, and while there were still three cubits to be cut through, [there was heard] the voice of a man calling to his fellows, for there was an overlap in the rock on the right [and on the left]. And when the tunnel was driven through, the quarrymen hewed (the rock), each man toward his fellow, axe against axe, and the water flowed from the spring toward the reservoir for 1,200 cubits, and the height of the rock above the head(s) of the quarrymen was 100 cubits."*

*(right)* "**David's Palace.**" *Since excavations began in 1880 on the hill of the City of David, there were no finds of a structure that could be identified with any mentioned in early literary sources. However, during the excavations carried out on the crest of the City of David, at the point where the hill's shoulders are narrowest and the northern fortifications should have been built, remains of a large public building dating from the eleventh to tenth centuries BCE were uncovered. It was immediately suggested that this may have been the remains of the Zion stronghold where King David resided and renamed "the City of David" (2 Sam. 5:9). This suggestion has not yet been substantiated.*

*The* **terraced structure** *built during the Late Bronze (fourteenth to thirteenth centuries BCE) or Iron Age I (twelfth to eleventh centuries BCE) at the northeastern end of the City of David. It was constructed by fills of stone and soil and reinforced by thin stone walls, forming an artificial tell. This tell constituted a base on which the acropolis of Canaanite Jerusalem was apparently built. (This was the fortified section of Jerusalem where the administrative buildings of the Canaanite and Jebusite city were situated.)*

*After conquering the city, King David reembellished this structure as a base for his palace. The Bible does not mention David building a palace. He used the palace of his predecessors (the Citadel of Zion which he renamed the City of David). To reinforce the structure, he encompassed it with a system of terraces, for additional support to the fillings. It is this complex which can still be seen on the site. The palace, which David used inside the enclosure created by the terraced structure, may well be that which Hiram, king of Tyre, helped to reembellish (2 Sam. 5:11), or it may be David's Citadel mentioned in the Bible (2 Sam. 5:9). In the course of time, when King Solomon built the administrative center of his kingdom on the Temple Mount, consisting of a palace and Temple, the palace used by David was no longer of any significance. The terraced structure, which had served as a basis for it, turned into a tell. On this tell, and on its edges, dwellings were constructed. The result was a complete change in the terraced structure. Only a small section is still visible, enabling us to appreciate the extent of the royal construction works during the reign of King David.*

*The terraced structure was newly examined during the City of David excavations that began in 1978. Although the structure had already been unearthed in the excavations carried out by Macalister and Duncan (1923–1925) and by Kenyon (1967–1968), its real significance was not appreciated at the time.*

made up of materials from the city itself (in which important finds were discovered) to create a surface on which more dwellings could be built.

The reconstruction of the topography of biblical Jerusalem is based on archaeological finds as well as verses in the Bible relating to various building projects within the city, and the boundaries within which it expanded. It was long considered that the Book of Nehemiah provided evidence of Jerusalem's urban structure during the First Temple period. However, from the excavations carried out in the City of David, which began in the 1960s, it became evident that the city's dimensions were greatly reduced in the time of Nehemiah when compared with those of the First Temple period, and the direction of the city walls changed accordingly. As few sources have remained (such as the descriptions in the Book of Nehemiah), it is impossible to reconstruct the topographical continuity of the area.

The third phase of Jerusalem's urban development apparently began during Uzziah's reign, in the mid-eighth century BCE. This king is referred to in the Bible as having reinforced the walls of Jerusalem and as having built its towers: "Moreover Uzziah built towers in Jerusalem at the corner gate, and at the valley gate, and at the turning of the wall, and fortified them" (2 Chron. 26:9). His son, Jotham, also continued to fortify the city (2 Chron. 27:3), and during this period—although there is no specific reference to it in the Bible—the city began to expand beyond its original dimensions.

The strengthening of Assyria, the destruction of the Kingdom of Israel in 722 BCE, the struggle between Judah and the coastal city-states for sovereignty over western Judah, and especially Sennacherib's siege of the towns of Judah, brought a stream of refugees to Jerusalem who settled in the area within the city walls and the vicinity.

*(below)* **Reconstruction of the entrance to the Tell Ta'yinat temple**, *with its two pillars supporting the entrance roof. There is a great similarity between this temple and the Temple in Jerusalem as described in the Bible. The two pillars in this illustration recall Jachin and Boaz—the two pillars mentioned in the Bible (2 Chron. 3:17; 1 Kings 7:21). Lions such as those supporting the pillars are found in Syrian architecture, and were not used in the Jerusalem Temple. The illustration shows how impressive the entrance to the temple was.*

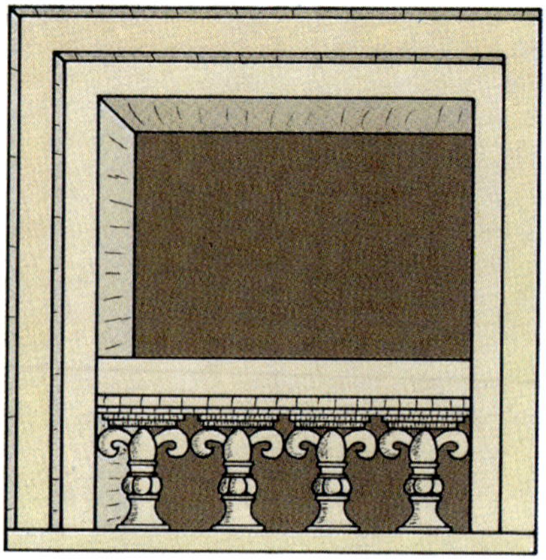

*(above)* **Reconstruction of a window frame** *with decorations carved in stone from the First Temple period found at Ramat Rahel. The remains were in part decorated in relief and part sculpted, and apparently belonged to more than one window, which is a reflection of the quality of the structure. It is certain that this was a royal palace built in the ninth century BCE (during the reign of Asa or Jehoshaphat).*

*The reconstruction of the window, as illustrated here, is based on a similar structure found on ivory panels dating to the same period in other places such as Calah (Nimrud) in Assyria.*

*The discovery of the palace in the vicinity of Jerusalem is evidence of the means of the royal family in Judah, and the sources of cultural influence upon them.*

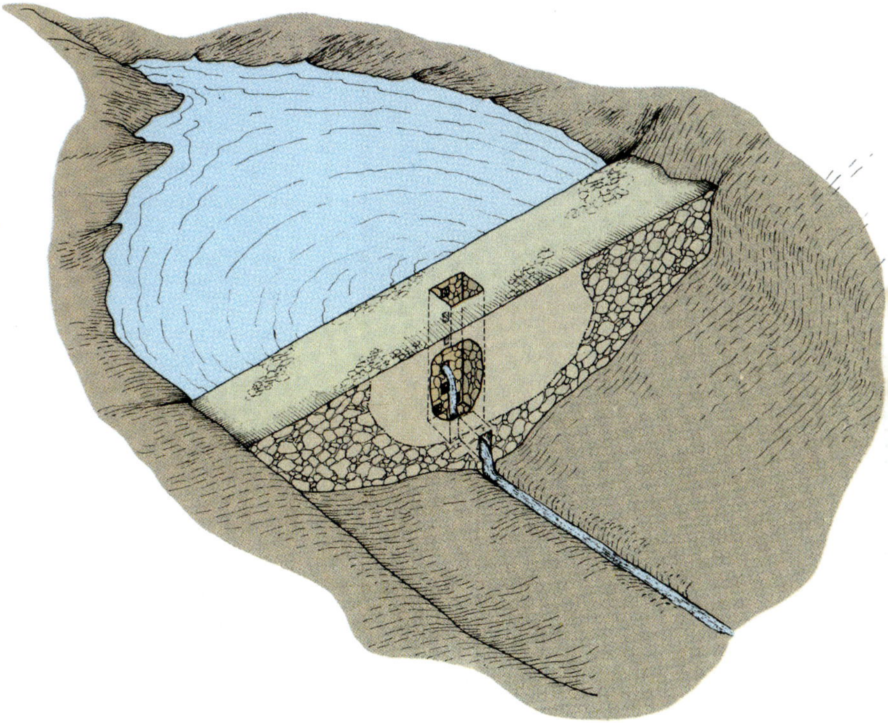

*Toward the end of the kingdom of Judah a large* **dam** *was built across the* **Beth Zetha Valley** *on the site where in the Second Temple period the* **Sheep's Pools** *were located (today in the courtyard of the Church of St. Anne). The dam was about 131 feet (40 m) long, 20 feet (6 m) broad in its upper section and 23 feet (7 m) in the lower section, and 43 feet (13 m) high. It formed a pool which retained the waters flowing along the Beth Zetha Valley southward. This pool is situated above the second pool, to the south, and they were created at different times.*

*At the center of the dam a square shaft was built (3×3 feet [1×1 m]); openings (6×8 inches [15×20 cm]) were made in it every 6.5 feet (2 m) connecting the shaft with the upper pool (the northern one). At the base of the shaft were two apertures the height of the base of the pool. These apertures served to regulate the draining of the waters from the pool toward the south.*

*It appears that the function of the dam was to accumulate the waters so as to control their flow into a conduit that conducted the waters to east of the Temple Mount, along its contour into the area of the Ophel (where its continuation was found carved out of the rock) and to the hill of the upper city, which became part of the city in Hezekiah's time. A section of this conduit, about 164 feet (50 m) long, that ran from the dam to the south has been unearthed. It is 3 feet (1 m) deep and 30 inches (75 cm) wide. The scholars who discovered the conduit are of the opinion that the waters flowed from the pool to the conduit in the direction of the Temple, and were used by the people working in it. These facts were derived from the archaeological excavations carried out at the site by the owners of the land area, members of the Order of the White Fathers.*

**Iron arrowheads** *from the time of the destruction of Jerusalem by Nebuchadnezzar (586 BCE) discovered in the archaeological excavations in the Jewish Quarter. Flat arrowheads were found in the stratum of burnt materials (charred wood, ashes, and soot) at the foot of the remains of a high tower from the Iron Age. One of the arrowheads was a Scythian arrow made of bronze, which was brought to the land of Israel by conquering armies from the seventh century BCE. It would seem that during the attack on the city, flaming torches hurled by the conquerors set the buildings on fire. The siege of the tower and the tumult during the attempts to take it were indicative of the events in Jerusalem during the days preceding the destruction of the First Temple.*

*The* **Siloam Tunnel**. *In the nineteenth century, it became evident that on the hill of the City of David there were installations built to supply water to the Siloam Pool. Great work was done in the eighteenth century* BCE, *when the Gihon Spring, located outside the city, was fortified and its waters were diverted to a nearby pool. An aqueduct was also cut out of the rock for some hundreds of meters in length, ending in the pool. The channel is very narrow, with room for only a single person to pass along its breadth. The winding tunnel is interspersed with small openings, exposing it to daylight. When the level of the water in the spring dropped to a point where it could no longer be channeled, the tunnel fell into disuse and was abandoned for about a thousand years. King Hezekiah then replaced it with his renowned rock-cut tunnel.*

Thus, for example, remains of dwellings have been discovered outside the city, in area B of the City of David excavations, in the area of Mount Zion, and on the western slopes of the Old City facing the Sultan's Pool.

The events described above occurred during the long reign of King Hezekiah (727–698 BCE), and were the motive for his great construction projects in Jerusalem, such as the new wall which also encompassed the new quarters established during this period outside the walls (Isa. 22:10; 2 Chron. 32:5), and the excavation of the tunnel which brought water from the Gihon Spring to the Siloam Pool inside the city (2 Kings 20:20). Nineteenth-century scholars and laymen alike identified this tunnel as having been built by King Hezekiah.

The wall built by Hezekiah was discovered by Prof. Avigad during his excavations in the Jewish Quarter. According to the archaeological findings, the course of the wall was based on the network of dry riverbeds in the city. The buildings constructed along the newly built wall alignment were pulled down to enable the wall to be built. Thus, in area A of the excavations of the Jewish Quarter, a section of this wall was found, on both sides of which were remains of buildings pulled down during its construction, as described in Isaiah: "And ye have numbered the houses of Jerusalem, and the houses have ye broken down to fortify the wall" (22:10). Thus it can be assumed that the wall discovered in the Jewish Quarter is a section of the wall built by Hezekiah as protection against the siege of Jerusalem by Sennacherib, king of Assyria, in 701 BCE. It has not been possible to determine the exact function of two additional sections of the fortifications found in the vicinity (area S and area 11 of the excavations) within the complex of fortifications of that period. It may well be that they are part of the city's fortifications from a later period, during the time of Manasseh. Avigad also considered them to be a four-chambered city gate, as was customary of the period, the building of which was intended to improve the northern fortification line of the new city's quarters.

According to the Bible (2 Chron. 33:14), Manasseh fortified the city during his long reign over Judah (697–643 BCE), and the construction of the wall was one of his more important undertakings. A section of Hezekiah's wall was uncovered by Kathleen Kenyon during her excavations on the eastern slopes of Mount Zion, near the Siloam Pool.

The controversy over the city's dimensions during the First Temple period, which continued from the beginning of the exploration of Jerusalem, was brought to an end with the discovery of this wall. Many scholars were convinced that Jerusalem's boundaries were the hill of the City of David and the Temple Mount. Other scholars believed that the city was much larger, and that its western boundary passed through the area of the present-day Old City. This would mean that the city was situated on the hill which today encompasses the Jewish and Armenian Quarters as well as Mount Zion. The excavations in the Jewish Quarter have established that the city did expand beyond its earlier boundaries, but this

# The Temple at Tell Ta'yinat

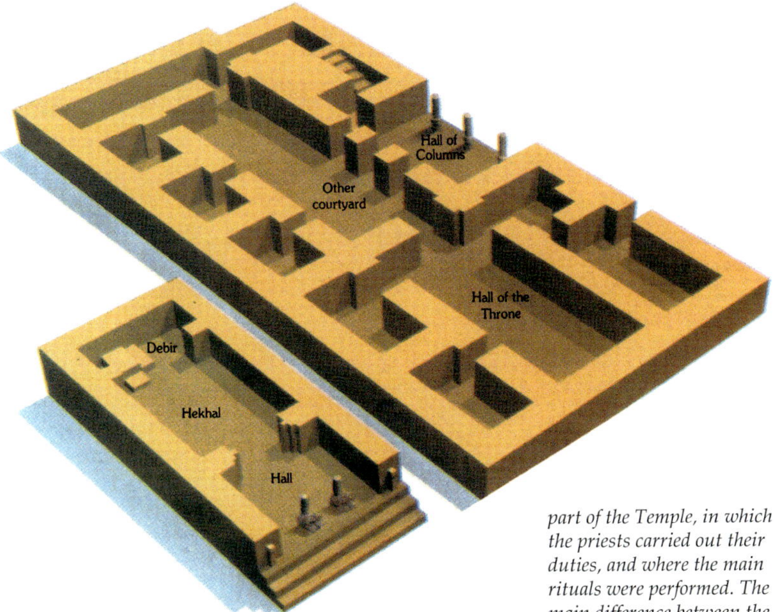


*The* **Temple at Tell Ta'yinat**. *The construction of the Temple in Jerusalem was certainly one of the pinnacles of building during the First Temple period. The biblical books of Kings and Chronicles give detailed descriptions of the construction of the Temple and hardly relate to the palace adjacent to it. Both the comparison of building projects from this period in neighboring countries and our conception of the fortification of the Temple Mount lead to the conclusion that the organization of the administrative area was based on the proximity between the Temple and the royal palace. A good example of this is seen in the illustration of the administration complex at Tell Ta'yinat and the* **temple of Ein Dara** *(below, right) in northern Syria. This structure also confirms the biblical descriptions, and adds to our understanding of the complex built by King Solomon on the Temple Mount. Although the Tell Ta'yinat complex post-dates King Solomon's reign by about two centuries, it enables us to learn about the structure of the various sections of a royal palace, and the size of the palace in relation to the temple. It should be pointed out that the location of some other administration complexes of the type shown here is unknown. For example, the First Book of Kings mentions the "house of the forest of Lebanon" (7:2) and the house of "Pharaoh's daughter" (9:24). The Bible also states that Solomon built his palace over a period of thirteen years, and the Temple in only six years (1 Kings 7:1). This fact shows that both from the point of view of time and of magnitude, the building of the palace exceeded the construction of the Temple.*

*Palaces of the style of this edifice have been found in the excavations at Megiddo, in the levels from the reign of Solomon, and the following elements can be discerned: the hall of columns (which served as a vestibule), an inner courtyard (termed in the Bible the "other courtyard," and which was the living area of the king and his retinue), and a large hall which is the "hall of the throne" mentioned in the Bible. The broad walls shown in the illustration were, according to the Bible, to be found in the royal palace in Jerusalem. The temple itself, whose interior measurements were 20×70 cubits (approximately 33×115 feet [10×35 m]), faced toward the east, and the function of the front hall reached by a stairway, was to separate the courtyard from the sanctuary (Hekhal) itself. It would seem that in the Tell Ta'yinat temple the pillars which stood on the backs of lions fulfilled the function of the biblical pillars of Jachin and Boaz (1 Kings 7:21). From the hall, an entrance led to the sanctuary, the main part of the Temple, in which the priests carried out their duties, and where the main rituals were performed. The main difference between the Tell Ta'yinat temple and the Temple in Jerusalem was the length of the innermost section, the inner sanctuary (Debir) where the holy ark and the cherubim were situated. In Jerusalem this was twenty cubits in length while in Tell Ta'yinat it was only ten cubits. The Tell Ta'yinat sanctuary was thus twice as long as the inner sanctuary of the Jerusalem Temple.*

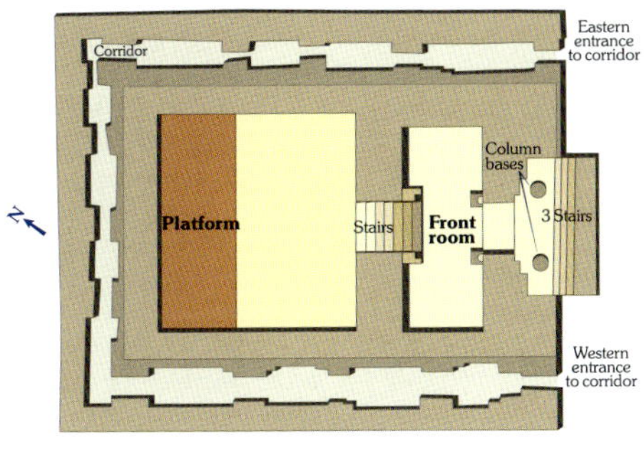

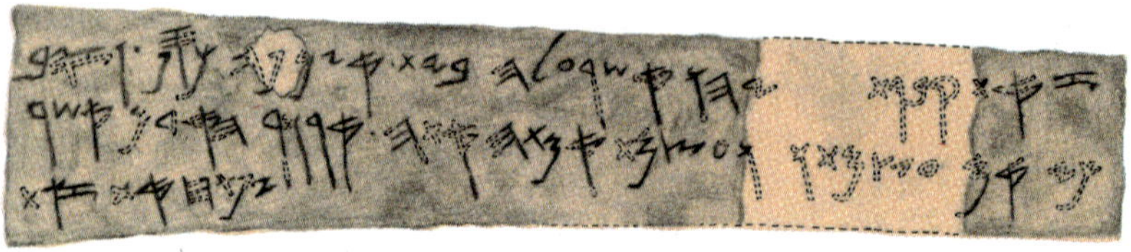

*Two* **tomb inscriptions** *discovered by the French scholar Charles Clermont-Ganneau in 1870 in the village of Siloam, near Jerusalem. These inscriptions are from one of the most elaborate tombs found in this area, where there is the largest concentration of tombs from the First Temple period in biblical Jerusalem. The larger inscription reads: "This is the tomb of . . . Yahu who is over the house. There is no silver and no gold here, only his bones and the bones of his slave wife (who is) with him. Cursed be he who will open this." It would seem that this is the tomb of a nobleman, and it is certainly possible that the remaining letters of the inscription—*yod, heh, vav*—are the final letters of the name Shebna which appears in Isaiah: "Go, get thee unto this treasurer, even unto Shebna, which is over the house, and say, What hast thou here? and whom hast thou here, that thou hast hewed thee out a sepulchre here, as he that heweth him out a sepulchre on high, and that graveth an habitation for himself in a rock?" (22:15–16). The second inscription was found carved in the rock at the entrance to another chamber nearby. The inscription reads:* heder be-katef ha-tzur, *meaning "a room behind the rock," or another interpretation,* heder be-katef ha-tzariah, *meaning "a room behind the cave." Both these versions show that it was the intention of the builders of the tomb to warn builders of other tombs that in addition to the large burial chamber there was another chamber, and therefore they should not excavate in that vicinity.*

*The* **Tomb of Pharaoh's Daughter** *in the village of Siloam, is called thus because of a tradition popular among the Arabs of the region that any strange phenomenon that occurs has to be connected to Pharaoh. Thus, for example, the "Absalom's Pillar" in the same area is called in Arabic "Pharaoh's Headdress." The biblical description of the house of Solomon's wife—Pharaoh's daughter—made it easier for the Jews to accept the designation "Tomb of Pharaoh's Daughter" (2 Kings 9:24).*

*This is a nobleman's tomb, expertly constructed. The structure underwent many changes during the Byzantine period, when a cell was hewn out to serve as a dwelling for monks. Furthermore, the pyramid on its roof was taken down for the use of the stone, the small opening was enlarged toward the lintel, and the inscription carved above the original opening was removed. Only two letters have remained—*vav *and* reish*. They may possibly be the final letters of the word* arur *(cursed) which was part of the sentence, "cursed be he who opens this grave," an inscription found on other tombs in this area from the First Temple period.*

occurred only at the end of the eighth century BCE. The many finds from the excavations in Jerusalem, including various kinds of inscriptions, add information which connect these finds to the Bible, and testify to the city's strength from the eighth to sixth centuries BCE.

Some scholars are now of the opinion that the course of the First Temple period wall is identical to that of the First Wall from the Second Temple period. They argue that proof of this is provided by Josephus Flavius, who states that the First Wall was built during the rule of David and Solomon and the kings who reigned after them (*Wars* 5, 4, 1). They also base their argument on the fact that the remains discovered of the First Temple period walls were adjacent to the First Wall. But since Josephus himself (*Antiquities* 10, 44) relates that Manasseh built a citadel in the upper city, one can assume that the wall passed through what is now the Street of the Jews, since it is traversed by a riverbed that could have served as the wall's foundation. It is within this area, the present-day Jewish Quarter, that a relatively dense settlement existed during the First Temple period, and perhaps a citadel stood on the western side of the hill where the present Citadel now stands.

The discovery of only a few houses within the confines of the Armenian Quarter and Mount Zion, as compared with a larger number of houses found in the Jewish Quarter, indicates that the situation there was similar to that which existed in the City of David (area B). In that area, too, a

**Burial caves in the courtyard of the St. Etiénne monastery.** *At the end of the nineteenth century when the Church of St. Etiénne (St. Stephen's Church) was rebuilt, two large burial caves were discovered in the courtyard. The archaeologist who excavated them did not date them accurately, and only in the course of time when the type of burial cave dating to the end of the First Temple period was identified (eighth to seventh centuries BCE) it became apparent that these burial caves belonged to a necropolis in the north of the city from this period. Characteristic of this type of tomb was the burial chamber which generally contained three shelves laid around its walls (excluding the entrance side). The corpse was placed on the shelf with its head resting in a recess in the form of a pillow hewn out of the rock. Some of these "pillows" were formed in the style of the hair of the Egyptian goddess Hathor. A further decoration in the cave was a cornice which ran along the length of the chamber walls where they join up with the ceiling. The majority of the burial chambers had pits used as receptacles for bones (the bones of the dead buried earlier were placed in them to make room for other bodies). Three stairs led to the shelf above the opening and it would seem that this was the most distinguished shelf of the three in the chamber. The second burial chamber, which is not described here, now serves as a burial cave for monks. Some renowned scholars of Palestine have also been buried here, such as Father F. M. Abel, Father L. H. Vincent, Father R. de Vaux, and Father P. Benoit, Father M. J. Lagrange and others.*

*These two caves are among the most beautiful First Temple period burial caves discovered so far. Of late, conjecture has been put forward that these might be the caves referred to by Josephus as the "Royal Caves" (in his description of the Third Wall), but so far no proof has been found to support this theory. Other burial caves have been discovered north of Damascus Gate, thus showing that this was an accepted burial ground at the end of the First Temple period.*

**"This is the tomb ... who opens it"** *are the words of a Hebrew inscription carved in a rock, discovered in 1946 in the village of Siloam. The inscription was engraved above the facade of a First Temple burial cave hewn out of the rock. The villagers of Siloam sealed the cave and turned it into a water cistern, which still serves them to this day. The inscription, which was intact after the Six-Day War of 1967, has recently been despoiled by inhabitants of the village.*

number of the houses of the new settlers in Jerusalem were built outside the city walls. Support of the minimalist approach can also be found in the fact that nowhere other than in the Jewish Quarter have remains been discovered of the city wall which can definitely be dated to the First Temple period. The absence of such remains in the large area excavated in the grounds of the Citadel, and along the length of the western part of the Old City walls, reduces the plausibility of the maximalist approach. Even if remains are found outside the city, this will not refute the minimalist determination of the city's boundaries.

In the northern part of the present-day Old City, remains have been found which cast light upon the expansion of the city in this direction. In the vicinity of the Muristan and the Church of the Holy Sepulcher, remains of quarries dating to this period have been found, and it would appear that they were situated outside the city confines. The assumption that many installations of the city were outside its walls is reinforced by the discovery that the northernmost of the two Sheep's Pools (the Bethesda Pools) was also built about the time of Hezekiah, when a dam was erected across the Beth Zetha Valley to catch the floodwaters from this valley. An opening was made in this dam for draining off waters to a conduit, which would seem to be the conduit known from the time of the Assyrian siege: "They came and stood by the conduit of the upper pool, which is in the highway of the fuller's field" (2 Kings 18:17). The biblical description of Sennacherib's siege would seem to infer that the people besieged within the city were located to the north of the Temple Mount in the vicinity of the conduit branching off the dam. In recent excavations more proof as to the size of the city was revealed, when a large building in the Western Wall Plaza area was uncovered along with some *in situ* vessels found in the Western Wall tunnels.

A further source for comprehending the extent of the city's expansion is to be found in the cemeteries surrounding it. Until the Six-Day War in 1967, scholars were aware of the existence of a cemetery within the City of David and one in the village of Siloam. The graves in Siloam are a particularly good example of the method of burial employed in Jerusalem during the First Temple period. In the course of the excavations carried out at the Western Wall, additional graves from this period, to the purification of which perhaps Ezekiel (43:7–9) referred, were discovered west of Robinson's Arch. However, neither of these groups of graves has added to our knowledge of the city during the First Temple period, since geographically they were in close proximity to the hill of the City of David, and the connection between the graves and the hill was obvious.

It was only with the discovery of a group of graves in the north of the city, in the vicinity of the Damascus Gate and to the north of it, that the city had a magnificent necropolis, befitting a large and important city. Some of the graves unearthed in the north of the city—in the courtyard of the St. Etiénne (St. Stephen) Monastery—are the most magnificent yet found in Israel. It would appear that a number of graves from this period exists in the present-day Christian Quarter (one was found in the Coptic Patriarchate near the Holy Sepulcher), and others have been discovered on the city's western slopes in the direction of the Sultan's Pool. Another cluster of graves is located in the riverbed of the Valley of Hinnom, and a further one has been discovered on the hill on which St. Andrew's Church and the Begin Center now stand, where a rich crop of archaeological finds has been uncovered. A number of graves was unearthed some time ago in Mamilla Street. Thus it is clear that the necropolis extended over a large area of the city. Even if this fact alone does not assist us in determining the exact boundaries, the abundance of other findings throughout the city is proof of the city's magnitude during the two centuries prior to the destruction of the First Temple.

**Tombs Tl and T2.** *In the excavations carried out in the City of David in 1913–1914, R. Weill uncovered stone quarries from the Roman period. These quarries damaged some areas of the City of David, then outside the boundaries of the Roman city. Many remains were found from the pre-Roman period which had been badly damaged by the quarrying. Among these finds were two artificially cut caves which Weill believed were the tombs of the kings of the Davidic dynasty. Very little has remained of that named T2, while there are enough remains of T1 to reconstruct the outlines of the tomb.*

*Weill believed that there were two stages to the building of the tomb. In the first stage a passageway was excavated 52.5 feet (16 m) long, the entrance to which was in the south. Near the northern end of the passageway, slightly above floor level, a niche was made into which the corpse was placed (or perhaps the sarcophagus). The passageway was then sealed off with stone slabs. Triangular niches were made in the wall along the passageway for candles, a fact which confirms the multiple use of the site. In the course of time, the necropolis became overcrowded, a fact that is borne out by the Bible which describes the burial place of the first kings of the Davidic dynasty thus: "And he was laid to rest with his fathers in the City of David." The later description of the burial place was the "City of David" and not "the sepulchre of the kings" (thus Jehoram and Joash). Later, the "Garden of Uzzah" is referred to as the burial place. In the second stage an additional passageway was dug and an additional opening was made under the forward section of the first passageway. Most of this opening remained, as well as the stairs that led to it. It appears that the new sarcophagus was placed at the end of the lower passageway, and obviously when this excavation was carried out, direct contact with the sarcophagus in the upper level was cut off. To this end incisions were made in the walls on both sides of the passageway which served to support a wooden dome upon which a new floor (also made of wood) to the upper passageway was laid.*

*As the site was turned into a quarry during the Roman period, and both parts of the passageway were broken into, all the accompanying objects in the tomb were stolen. Thus, we do not have any definitive proof of the use of this structure, its exact date, or whether this actually was the burial place of the kings of the Davidic dynasty.*

# The Second Temple Period

## 538 BCE – 70 CE

The Second Temple period lasted for over 600 years, from the Proclamation of Cyrus up to the destruction of the Second Temple. In the course of this period Jerusalem's image changed, and from a small partly destroyed settlement it became one of the most important and famous cities in the Orient.

This chapter of the city's history is divided into three sections: the times of Nehemiah, the Hasmoneans, and the period of the reign of the Herodian kings.

The map at the beginning of this chapter showing Jerusalem on the eve of its destruction by the Romans, refers to all three periods. It is based on archaeological findings, historical sources and an attempt to link them together. Sites which have not been conclusively identified appear on the map by name but with no exact placement.

### From the Return to Zion to the Hasmonean Period

After the destruction of the First Temple in 586 BCE Jerusalem was once again reduced to the area of the City of David and the Temple Mount. The western section (the Western Hill) was still surrounded by the remains of the city wall several feet in height, but the area within it apparently lay largely in ruins. According to the description in the Book of Nehemiah and archaeological finds, Jerusalem was a devastated city, and its demolished walls served as some sort of defense for its few inhabitants.

The Proclamation of Cyrus, given in 538 BCE, was the beginning of a process which brought about the restitution of the spiritual and political life of the Jews in their land. Cyrus gave permission for the Jews to return to Judea and to resurrect their Temple from its ruins. Twenty-two years later (516 BCE), the restored Temple was dedicated under the leadership of Jeshua son of Jehozadak and Zerubbabel son of Shealtiel. Huge amounts of money were contributed for the erection of the Second Temple, cedar wood was brought from Lebanon and stone masons and carpenters came from Tyre and Sidon to assist in the construction work. The dedication ceremony of the Second Temple was a grand and impressive event, and the priests and Levites once more began to carry out their holy duties and the rituals were resumed. Jerusalem, now the capital of the Persian province of Yehud, was once more the center of life in Judea. Evidence of this is found in the many seals from this period unearthed in archaeological excavations. Even so, it remained desolate for many years to come. From the time of the dedication of the Temple until the arrival of Ezra the Scribe (fifty-eight years later), Jerusalem was ruled by persons who did not leave their mark on the history of the city.

Ezra the Scribe, who held a high position at the court of Artaxerxes I, king of Persia, came to Jerusalem from Babylon in the year 457 BCE at the head of a column of returnees. On the basis of the authorization granted him by the king, Ezra strove to spread the Torah, to strengthen the faith of the Jews and to renew the ritual in the Temple. It was only when Nehemiah reached Jerusalem that their joint efforts resulted in the introduction of a comprehensive reform.

Nehemiah came to Jerusalem in 445 BCE and brought about a major change in the city. Soon after his arrival he realized that it was essential to restore the walls and quickly set about putting his plan into action. The description of his nocturnal reconnaissance of the condition of the fortifications tells us of the course of the ruined walls. He began his rounds by leaving by the Valley Gate at the northwest of the City of David. From there he walked along the Tyropoeon Valley to the Dragon Well (probably En Rogel; according to this designation, the Dung Gate would be situated in the vicinity of the Siloam Pool). From the Dragon Well he turned in an easterly direction, climbed the western slopes of the Kidron Valley and looked down upon the ruined city walls lying halfway down the slope. From the northeastern corner of the City of David he turned to the west and went down the Tyropoeon Valley and returned to the Valley Gate.

The Jewish inhabitants labored fifty-two days to restore the walls of Jerusalem. Their enemies—

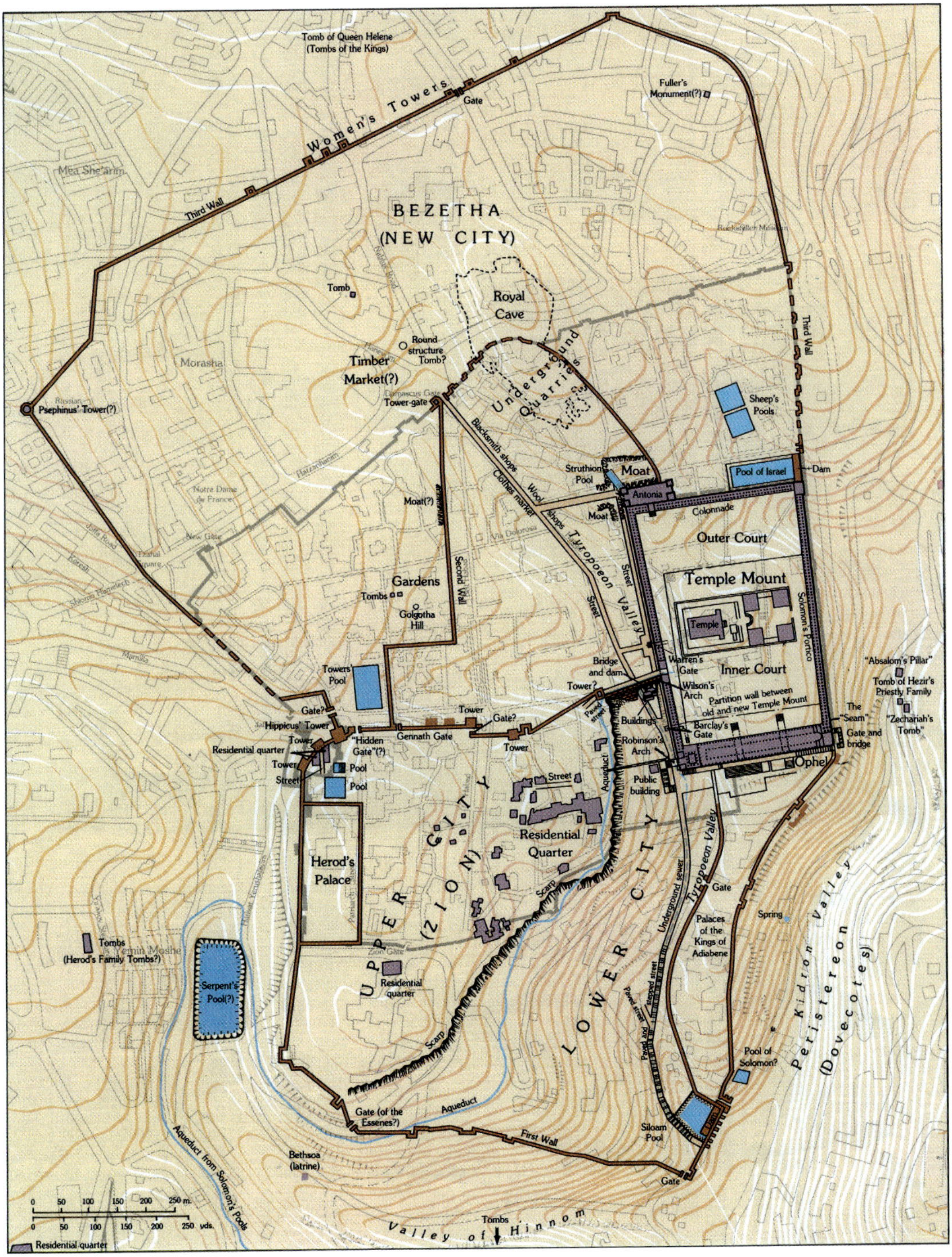
Tomb of Queen Helene (Tombs of the Kings)
Women's Towers
Gate
Fuller's Monument(?)
Mea She'arim
Third Wall
BEZETHA (NEW CITY)
Tomb
Royal Cave
Round structure Tomb?
Timber Market(?)
Morasha
Underground Quarries
Psephinus' Tower(?)
Damascus Gate
Tower-gate
Sheep's Pools
Blacksmith shops
Clothes market
Wool shops
Struthion Pool
Moat
Pool of Israel
Dam
Antonia
Moat(?)
Colonnade
Outer Court
Notre Dame de France
Tyropoeon Valley
Street
Temple Mount
Second Wall
Gardens
Tombs
Golgotha Hill
Temple
Solomon's Portico
Bridge and dam
Warren's Gate
Inner Court
"Absalom's Pillar"
Tomb of Hezir's Priestly Family
Towers Pool
Tower?
Wilson's Arch
Partition wall between old and new Temple Mount
The "Seam"
"Zechariah's Tomb"
Gate?
Tower
Hippicus' Tower
Barclay's Gate
Gate and bridge
Residential quarter
"Hidden Gate"(?)
Gennath Gate
Buildings
Robinson's Arch
Ophel
Pool
Public building
Street
Herod's Palace
UPPER CITY (ZION)
Residential Quarter
Aqueduct
Scarp
Tombs (Herod's Family Tombs?)
Yemin Moshe
Serpent's Pool(?)
Zion Gate
Residential quarter
LOWER CITY
Underground sewer
Gate
Palaces of the Kings of Adiabene
Spring
Kidron Valley
Peristereon (Dovecotes)
Pool of Solomon?
Gate (of the Essenes?)
Aqueduct
First Wall
Siloam Pool
Aqueduct from Solomon's Pools
Bethsoa (latrine)
Gate
Valley of Hinnom
Tombs
0 50 100 150 200 250 m.
0 50 100 150 200 250 yds.
Residential quarter

# Map of Jerusalem in the Time of Nehemiah

*A coin inscribed with the name* **Yehud**. *Coins of this type, in silver or bronze, were minted in the country in the fourth or beginning of the third century* BCE. *On one side there was an eagle with outspread wings, an owl or some other winged animal, as well as the inscription Yehud. It appears that the coins were minted in Jerusalem which was the capital of the province of Judea at that time. However, the coin does not show any particular connection to the city, nor does it have any typically Jewish symbols. Similar coins were minted in Judea at the beginning of the Hellenistic period bearing the image of Ptolemy I, who ruled over the country from 301 to 258* BCE.

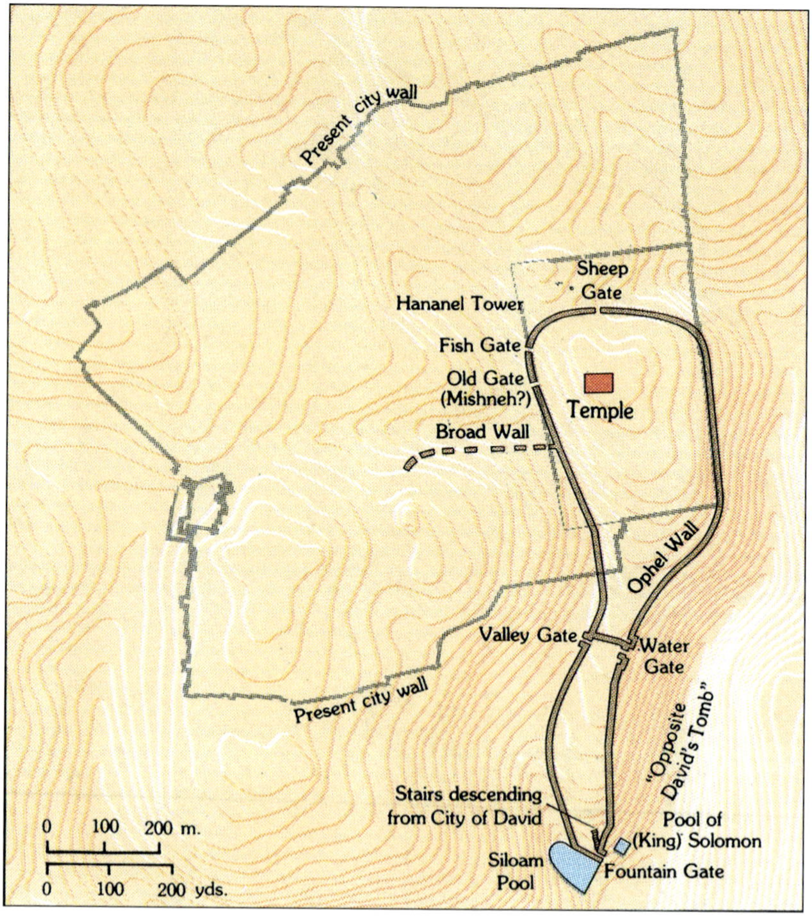


**Map of Jerusalem in the time of Nehemiah** *based on verses in the Book of Nehemiah (2:12–15; 3:1–33; 12:31–39) and archaeological discoveries made in the City of David, especially those relating to the city wall during this period.*

*The course of the city wall presented here is based on that of the First Temple period wall, and the names are those mentioned in the Book of Nehemiah. Even though the First Temple period walls are not completely identical with those of Nehemiah's time, there was no significant change in certain sections, such as was made on the Temple Mount. The references in the Book of Nehemiah, and especially those describing the erection of the wall, make it possible to identify various sites, but in this map we have marked only those places which can be reasonably identified* in situ. *Thus, for example, the Water Gate mentioned in Nehemiah (12:37) was found in the City of David, in the area above the Gihon Spring. This was at the site of the Old Gate which had been demolished at the time of the destruction of the First Temple. Since a new wall was built in Nehemiah's time and no gate was found in that region, the location of the Water Gate has been marked at the spot where the remains were found.*

the Ammonites, Arabians, and Ashdodites—who were living in the country at that time harassed the builders who were forced to defend themselves, as described in the Book of Nehemiah (4:17): "every one with one of his hands wrought in the work, and with the other hand held a weapon." The labor was divided among the priestly families, the inhabitants of the towns and villages in Judea, and the noble families in Jerusalem, and each group was assigned a section of the wall to be built or restored. The order of the sections enables us to trace the course of the wall at the time of its restoration. However, only a few sites along the wall have been identified conclusively. Among these are the Broad Wall, the Valley Gate, the Dung Gate, the Fountain Gate, the wall of the Siloam Pool, and the slopes of the City of David. Upon the completion of the building, a ceremony was held to mark the event, and the celebrants circled the restored walls in two columns—one came down from the Temple Mount to the City of David and passed the Dung Gate, the ascent to the City of David, the Water Gate, and other sites. The second column circled the city in the opposite direction and they converged at the Temple Mount.

*The eastern section of the* **First Wall** *and its* **two towers** *in area G of the City of David. The two towers were discovered by Macalister and Duncan during their archaeological excavations of this site in 1923. They named this site the "Jebusite Bastion." From the excavations carried out here by Kenyon and Shiloh, it is now obvious that these are the remains of Hasmonean fortifications, even though Hasmonean-style cut stone such as those from the northern or western section of this wall have not been found. The Book of Maccabees makes reference to the fact that restoration work was carried out on the walls of Jerusalem on a number of occasions by the Hasmonean rulers. In addition, we find that the style of building is not always identical. This leads us to the conclusion that certain sections of the wall were built at different times. The illustration shows the glacis which was laid by the Hasmoneans, built of sloping layers of soil and limestone laid in a manner which prevented the enemy from reaching the structure's foundations. The glacis concealed the terraced structure and the remains of the First Temple period buildings.*

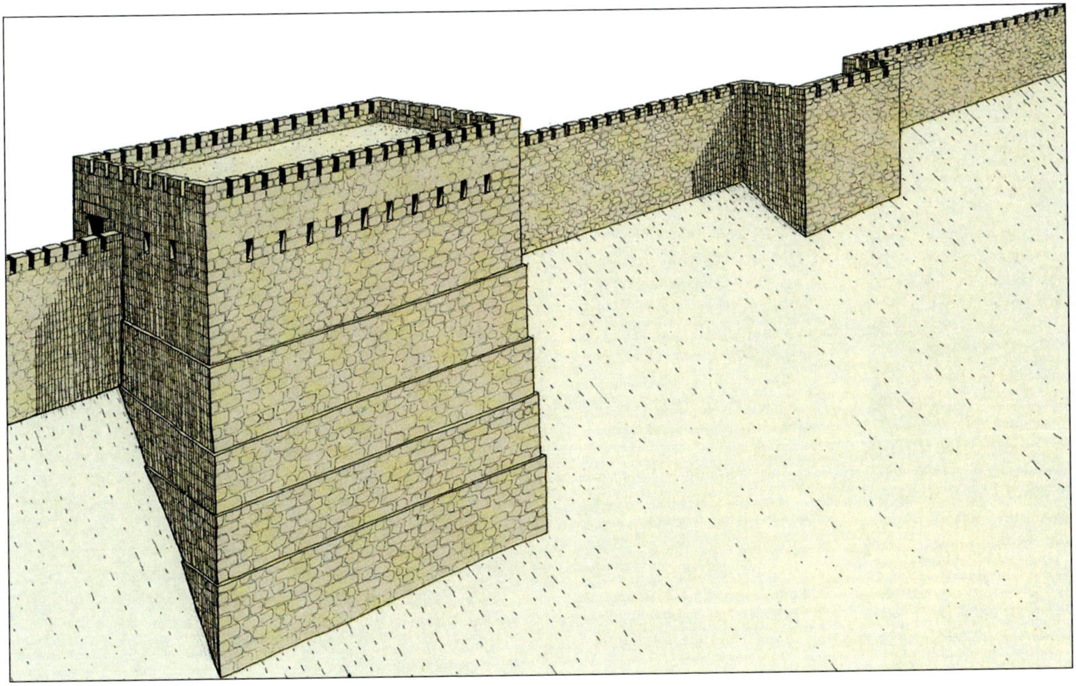

*In his description of the First Wall which surrounded the Upper City, Josephus states that the northeastern wall ended in the vicinity of the western portico of the Temple Mount, in the direction of the* **Council Building**. *This building was generally identified with the* **Chamber of Hewn Stones**, *mentioned in the sources, which was situated in the vicinity of the Temple Mount. (In the late Ottoman period, Jerusalem Jews used the name Chamber of Hewn Stones to refer to the Mahkama, a Mamluk building situated to the west of the Temple Mount, near the Gate of the Chain.)*

*In the course of his excavations in Jerusalem between 1867 and 1869, Warren discovered a hall near Wilson's Arch which he named the* **Hall of the Freemasons**. *The illustration presented here is a reconstruction of the hall based on the remains found there. In the Second Temple period the ceiling was flat and not vaulted as it is today.*

*The magnificent architectural style and its resemblance to other buildings from the Herodian era make it possible to date the hall to this period. The capitals have been reconstructed here as copies of the capital situated in the far right corner, which has remained intact. An additional pillar, apparently added during the Middle Ages, is situated in the middle of the hall (not reproduced here).*

*It seems that this was not the council building that existed in Jerusalem in the Second Temple period, but it undoubtedly served some public function. Hardly any vestiges of Second Temple period building in Jerusalem of such grandeur have remained, and this hall is a unique example of the high standard of architecture in the city during this period. To its west and connected by a corridor, there was discovered another hall identical in size, both of which probably formed a large public complex of unknown function.*

**A Hasmonean period residential quarter** *found underneath Herodian dwellings in one of the corners of the Citadel. The houses in this quarter were built close to the city wall, and the direction they faced was contingent upon the course of the wall. When Herod ascended the throne the entire region underwent a major change. The Hasmonean period roofs were removed, and the rooms filled up with earth. These earth-filled foundations served as the basis for a new residential quarter, facing in the general direction of the recently built houses. Herod's palace was built to the south and to the north of the Hippicus Tower, today called David's Tower. Following the destruction of the Second Temple, the Tenth Roman Legion encamped on this site.*

Even after the restoration of the walls, the city's population remained small: "Now the city was large and great: but the people were few therein, and the houses were not builded" (Neh. 7:4). The restoration of the walls was of greater importance than the provision of physical defense of the city's inhabitants. The fortifications enhanced Jerusalem's status as the nation's spiritual center, preserving its uniqueness and distinguishing it from the other peoples of the region. The description of the city in the Book of Nehemiah shows that in his time its dimensions were smaller than in the First Temple period. The new wall was built slightly to the east of the crest of the City of David, and as a result the eastern slope of the hill of the City of David and the wall enclosing it were not yet included within the boundaries of Jerusalem. We are still not certain of the course of the eastern wall in the time of Nehemiah. It is currently considered that the remains uncovered by Kathleen Kenyon, which she believed to be the ruins of the wall, are in fact remains of quarries and retaining walls built inside them. These remains are evidence of extensive construction works carried out throughout the entire city, and it is possible that it was from here that stone was quarried for the construction of the walls.

The descriptions of this period provide information about the walls only. There is almost

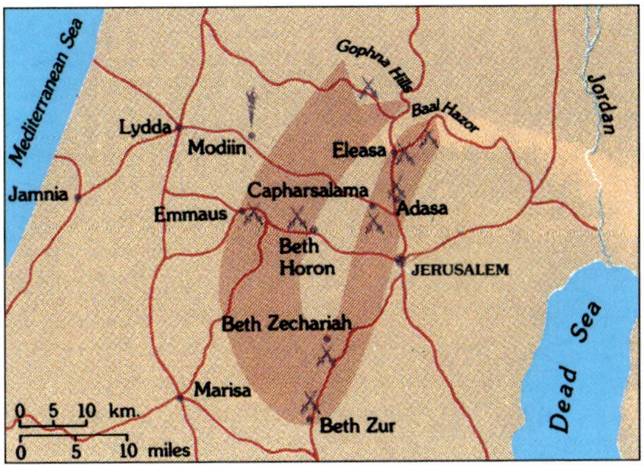


**Map** *showing the* **battles fought by the Maccabees** *to liberate Judea from the yoke of the Seleucids. The Hasmonean revolt began in Modiin, but the battles fought against the Seleucids and their allies, who sent reinforcements from outside Judea, began in the vicinity of the Gophna Hills. They then moved south to Beth Zur, and from there to the north, with Jerusalem as the focal point.*

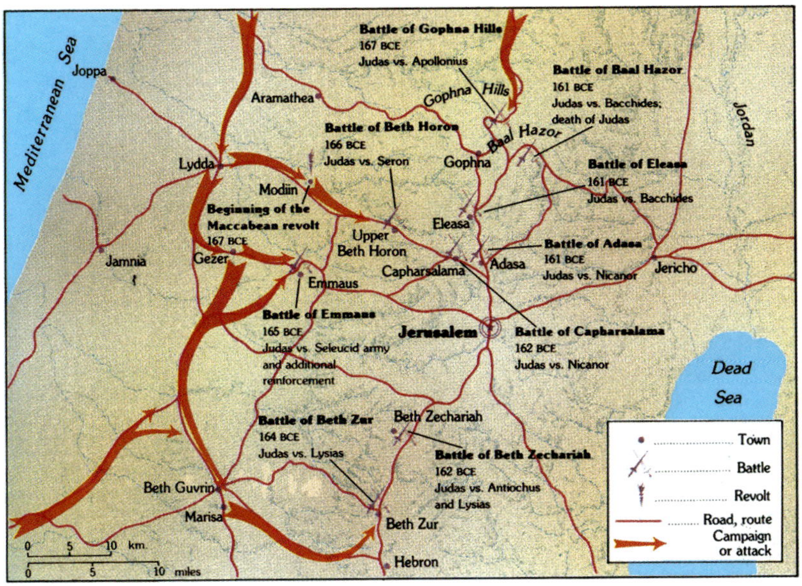


**Map of the battles for the liberation of Judea** *from the Seleucids. The Seleucid army was based in Jerusalem, and even though the battles took place some distance from the city, Jerusalem remained the focal point of the campaign.*

*The map shows the Hasmoneans' attempts to prevent the foreign forces reaching Jerusalem to join up with the Seleucids under siege in the Acra. The battles took place on the main routes leading to the city, and the Hasmonean strategy was to defend these routes. The map illustrates the vital role Jerusalem filled during the Second Temple period in general, and especially at the end of the Hasmonean era.*

no evidence available about other buildings or structures within the confines of the city itself. Apart from the houses of some local wealthy inhabitants mentioned in the Book of Nehemiah, a number of sites are referred to which can be identified with a certain amount of accuracy. These are the Broad Wall from the First Temple period, the Valley Gate, and the structures in the vicinity of the Siloam Pool (including the Dung Gate, the Fountain Gate, and the Siloam Pool wall). Another group of structures has been found to the north of the Temple Mount, among which were the Sheep Gate, the Mea Tower and the Hananel Tower. However, their exact location is unknown.

The hill of the City of David and the Temple Mount continued to be the focal points of the city. This is borne out by the abundance of archaeological finds dating to the fourth and third centuries BCE made in the City of David, in comparison with the scarcity of similar finds on the Western Hill. However, it would seem that the expansion in the direction of the Western Hill commenced prior to the Hasmonean period.

A number of sources, such as the Letter of Aristeas written in the third or the beginning of the second century BCE, provide evidence of extensive building projects in Jerusalem during that period. The largest of all was the erection or restoration of the Birah fortress (Baris in Greek), at the northwestern corner of the Temple Mount, on the site where the Antonia fortress was later built. The Birah fortress, with its many towers, kept guard over the Temple and its surroundings. Other building projects were bound up with the provision of water for the Temple, such as the underground water-supply system which brought water through conduits from the springs outside the city. It appears that at the same time the two Sheep's Pools were built (one was actually built during the First Temple period), renovations were made inside the Temple and on its paved forecourt, and the walls were reinforced.

The Book of Nehemiah, the Timocharus writings and the Letter of Aristeas are the only written historical records available relating to the history of Jerusalem from the Return to Zion up to the Hasmonean period, a period of approximately 350 years.

## The Hasmonean Period

The main source for the study of the Hasmonean period is provided by the Books of the Maccabees. Additional information is derived from archaeological excavations, as well as other sources.

The City of David area, which was inhabited at the end of the First Temple period, was aban-

*The* **Hasmonean period Citadel** *was situated in the northwest corner of the Upper City, after the area was annexed to Jerusalem in the late second century* BCE, *when the city expanded beyond the boundaries of the City of David. The First Wall built by the Hasmoneans passed through the Citadel (here it appears against the background of the present-day Citadel). The corner section reconstructed in the illustration shows the three Hasmonean towers (shaded) which underwent significant alterations during the period of Herod's rule (see the reconstructed model from that period on page 43).*

# Jerusalem in the Hasmonean Period

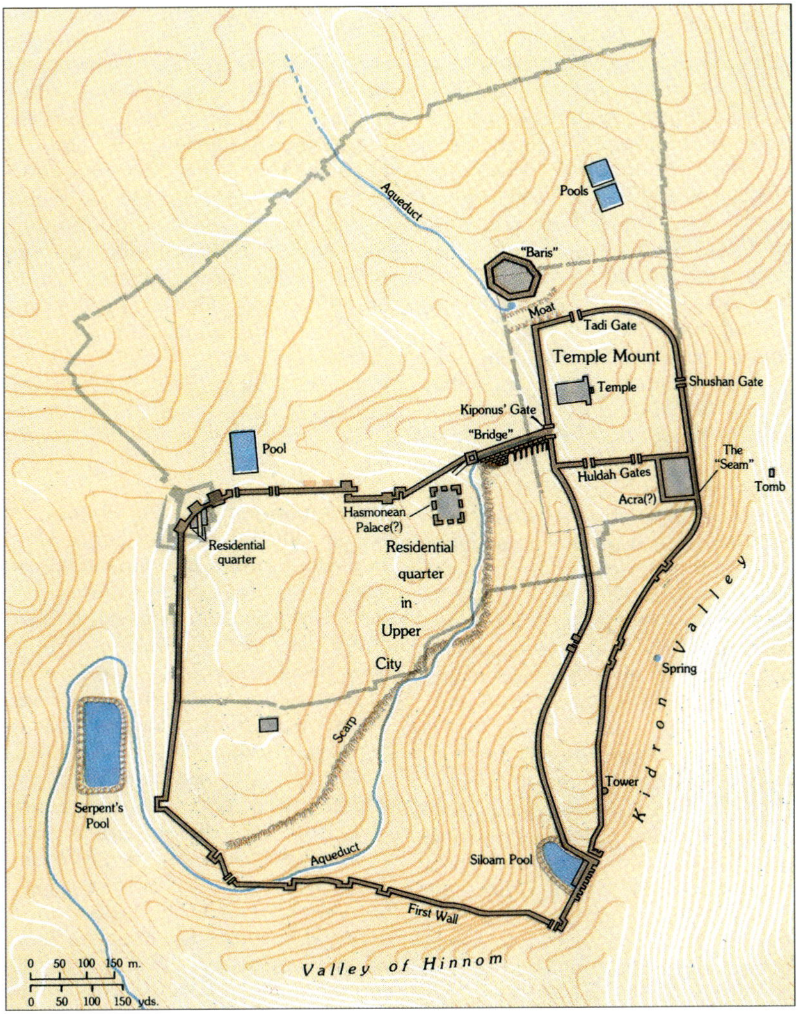


**Map of Jerusalem in the Hasmonean era** *showing only those sites whose location has been established beyond doubt based on the results of archaeological excavations carried out in the city. Structures from this period, known from historical sources only, have not been included in the map. Thus, for example, the built-up area within the present-day Jewish Quarter does not appear. The Hasmonean dynasty palace is delineated on the map in silhouette.*

*The course of the First Wall built by the Hasmoneans is one of the few details on the map which is not a matter of controversy. The location of the Temple Mount and the Baris has been definitively established, but their exact dimensions and shape during this period are still a matter of contention. The dimensions of the Hasmonean Temple Mount appear in the Mishnah (500×500 cubits), but the topography around the Temple Mount makes it impossible to conceive it as forming a complete square, but rather a square whose northeastern boundary is curved.*

*The location of the Acra is also a matter of controversy among scholars. It has been marked here according to one of the theories based on the findings in excavations carried out south of the Temple Mount.*

doned after the destruction of the Temple and remained desolate during the period of the Return to Zion. At the time of the outbreak of the Hasmonean revolt (167 BCE), Jerusalem was still confined within the boundaries of the City of David and the Temple Mount as it was in the days of Nehemiah. The beginning of Jerusalem's expansion to the west on the eve of the Hasmonean period was one of the most important milestones in its development. Apparently the First Temple period walls (such as the Broad Wall) were still visible above ground and served as the boundary for the renewed expansion of the city.

It is difficult to date with accuracy the beginning of the renewed settlement on the Western Hill, but it would appear that it commenced at the beginning of the second century BCE, after the victory of Antiochus III over the forces of the Ptolemies (200 BCE). It was during this period, under the rule of the Seleucid dynasty (whose center was in Antioch in northern Syria), that the struggle took place over the nation's spiritual image and for the control of Jerusalem. The penetration of Hellenistic culture into the country, and especially Jerusalem, was accelerated. Groups of Hellenizers who held positions of power assisted in this process, as manifested in the development of the Upper City area, which at the end of the Hasmonean period became Jerusalem's main urban center.

The greatest building project during the Hasmonean period was the construction of the wall that was called the Old Wall by Josephus (*Wars* 5, 4, 2). Archaeological excavations carried out at various sites in the city have provided proof that this wall was built in the middle of the second century BCE. This fact is supported by the Book of Maccabees (1, 10, 10), according to which Jonathan the Hasmonean began the construction of the city walls and building on Mount Zion. The project was continued by his brother Simon (Maccabees 1, 13, 1) and completed by his successor, John Hyrcanus I. The builders of this wall incorporated remains of the First Temple period wall, and perhaps this was the cause of Josephus' erroneous dating of the construction of the First Wall (the Old Wall) to the period of the Davidic dynasty.

It appears that the Hasmonean wall was built in stages. The first stage was apparently the erection of the wall in the western sector of the Western Hill. The eastern side was protected by a steep slope that was cut perpendicularly (its remains are still visible underneath the houses of the Jewish Quarter facing the Western Wall square). In light of the archaeological excavations which began at the site in 2006, the steep slope may have been cut into an escarpment only in the Roman or the Byzantine period, hence the question of the eastern defense of the Upper City remains unclear. This slope also protected the southern sector of the city until the completion of that wall section which began at the southernmost point of the City of David fortifications, near the Siloam Pool. This section ascended the western slopes of the Western Hill. The lack of uniformity in the building style, which can be seen in the sections themselves, is proof that it was not built at one time, and that various builders were involved in its construction.

## The Upper City

The erection of the First Wall during a period in which cultural-political processes took place in Jerusalem, as described in the Books of the Maccabees, raises two questions: what were the reasons for the expansion of the city to the Western Hill; and what was the character of the Upper City established there? One of the reasons for the city's expansion was probably the rising population density of the City of David. A further reason was the desire of the Hellenizers to make Jerusalem a Hellenistic city, and to this end a wider expanse was required. This was available on the Western Hill. Thus, during the Hasmonean period the Hellenistic style of building became predominant in the western sector of the city, especially in the houses of the rich. The finds from archaeological excavations uphold Josephus' accounts. In his writings mention is made of the Boulé (the city council building), the gymnasium and the Xystos (a courtyard surrounded by pillars which was generally attached to the gymnasium). These buildings are an integral part of every Hellenistic city. The Hasmoneans also built a palace in the Upper City, in the area overlooking the Temple Mount (*Wars* 2, 17, 3). Agrippa II embellished the palace and added a special wing from which he would look toward the Temple Mount (*Antiquities* 20, 89). Because of the lack of remains from this period it is difficult to present a complete picture of the Hellenistic city established on the Western Hill. One of the reasons for this was that

# Pompey's Siege of Jerusalem

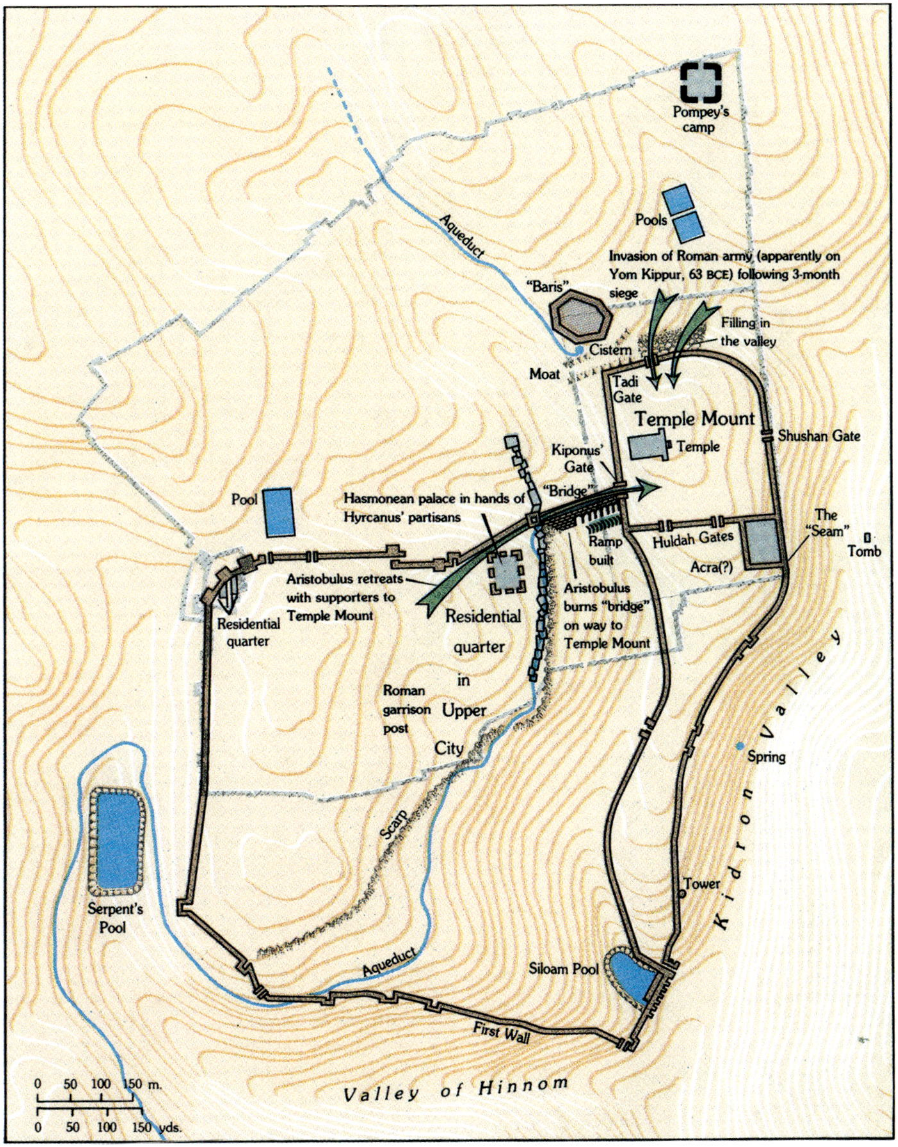


**Pompey's siege of Jerusalem** *in 63* BCE *lasted three months, until the city wall was finally breached. From the few references made by Josephus, we learn that Hyrcanus' men handed over the Upper City to Pompey. Thus the main effect of the siege and the thrust of the battle was concentrated around the Temple Mount. Apart from accounts of suicide carried out by civilians, who also set fire to their houses, there is no evidence of the conquest of the city's residential quarter, and it appears that the City of David was conquered only after the fall of the Temple Mount.*

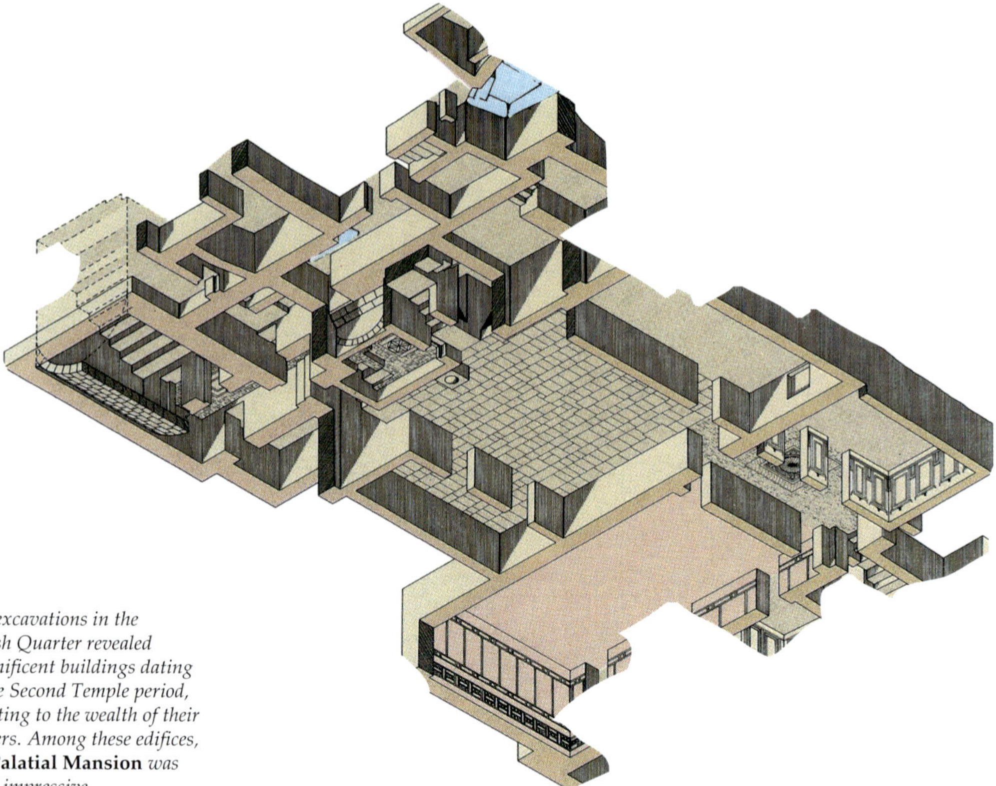

*The excavations in the Jewish Quarter revealed magnificent buildings dating to the Second Temple period, attesting to the wealth of their owners. Among these edifices, the* **Palatial Mansion** *was most impressive.*

*This structure was situated on the eastern slope of the Upper City where the escarpment descends to the Tyropoeon Valley and runs between a group of magnificent houses and the Temple Mount. The steep slope necessitated building at different levels: the lower level held the various water installations of the house—pools, ritual baths, and cisterns—as well as storerooms. The most embellished part of the building was situated at the second level. Despite topographic difficulties, the dimensions of the building were especially large, measuring approximately 600 square meters.*

*The main floor was built around a central paved courtyard, underneath which water cisterns were dug. A passageway led from the courtyard to the elaborate living quarters and the servants' quarters.*

*The building was embellished with mosaic floors, paneled plastering, colored plastering and paneled ceilings. Few remains were found inside the building, but they bear witness to the wealth of the owners. These included tables, glass vessels, earthenware utensils, and a sundial made from soft limestone.*

*This building, like large sectors of the quarter, was demolished during the destruction of Jerusalem in 70 CE, when the Upper City was taken and razed to the ground on the 5th of Elul that year.*

**Bronze coin from the time of Matthias Antigonus**, *last of the Hasmonean kings. Antigonus ruled from 40 to 37 BCE, during the period when the conflict between Herod and the Hasmoneans reached its climax. It may well be that as a result of this struggle many coins were minted during that period.*

*One side of the coin depicts the shewbread table surrounded by dots. Around the border is an inscription in Hebrew: "Matthias the High Priest." The inscription is distorted on most of the coins found and cannot be deciphered in the coin illustrated here.*

*On the obverse of the coin is the menorah (candelabrum) from the Temple, surrounded by an inscription in Greek: "King Antigonus." This inscription is also distorted.*

the city was rebuilt in Herod's time, and since the Herodian massive type of building required deep foundations, many buildings from the preceding Hasmonean period were pulled down and disappeared. Thus it can be seen that the Western Hill was settled in the Hasmonean period and played an important role in Jerusalem's urbanization up to the destruction of the Second Temple.

## The Temple Mount

There are no available sources for the description of the manner in which the Temple Mount was erected by the returnees to Zion. However, the Bible indicates the method was very poor (Ezra 3:12–13). The main development of the Temple Mount occurred in the third century BCE during the Hasmonean period.

The Temple Mount is described in the Mishnah (tractate *Middoth*), according to which the area measured 500×500 cubits. These measurements correspond largely with the excavations that were carried out in the Temple Mount area in the nineteenth century and from finds on the mount itself, mainly by Charles Warren (1867–1870).

Warren was able to determine the boundaries of Mount Moriah, the source of reverence for the Temple Mount. Converting the dome-shaped Mount Moriah into the Temple Mount required the building of four retaining walls, the eastern one of which is still seen today. The suggested date of this early Temple Mount is based on two written sources: the Letter of Aristeas and Ben-Sira's *Eccliasticus*. The date of these two works is a subject of controversy among scholars, but it is clear that their composition precedes the Hasmonean period.

The defined area of 500×500 cubits (c. 740×740 ft. / 225×225 m) is the area to which all the halakhic rules concerning the Temple Mount apply to this day, as it is preserved in the Mishnah. Apparently, this square area was known also in the time of Herod, with the expansion of the Temple Mount—thus Josephus' rendering of the "Inner Court" as opposed to the Herodian addition, which he calls the "Outer Court." An area of 250×250 meters is identical to that of Mount Moriah, whereas the Herodian Temple Mount known today measures 1,600 feet (488 m [western wall])×1,050 feet (320 m [northern wall]). This expansion was created in the course of Herod's monumental building projects, which included the digging of the Antonia hill, filling in part of the Tyropoeon Valley, elevating parts of the southern extension of Mount Moriah (at the southeastern end a subterranean structure may have been built, which later became "Solomon's Stables"), and the filling in of the Beth Zetha Valley and its western tributary, thus forming the Pool of Israel.

Josephus attributes some of the building works antedating Herod to the period of King Solomon and the Hasmonean period (*Wars* 5, 4, 1). There were five gates to the Temple Mount at this time: the two Huldah Gates (on the south), the Kiponus' Gate (west), the Tadi Gate (north), and the Shushan Gate (east). None of these gates has been identified, even though the Double Gate and Triple Gate visible today are erroneously called the Huldah Gates. The gates' names have all been designated to the area below the present-day Temple Mount.

Warren, during his excavations in the area of Wilson's Arch, discovered the stones of a bridge possibly constructed in the Hasmonean period, linking the Upper City with the Temple Mount. Josephus reports the destruction of this bridge in his *War of the Jews* (1, 7, 2): Aristobulus burned the bridge while retreating before Pompey, and he fled from the Upper City to the Temple Mount (63 BCE). This description reveals that the Temple Mount was the site of the last stand of the defenders of Jerusalem against the Romans. The site was fortified and its walls would seem to have been reinforced during the Hasmonean rule. Special mention must be made of the Baris fortress which existed already in Nehemiah's time (known then as the Birah) and was described in glowing terms in the Letter of Aristeas written on the eve of the Hasmonean era. According to Josephus, this fortress was built by kings of the Hasmonean dynasty (*Antiquities* 15, 403). Elsewhere he states: "When one of the priests, Hyrcanus I, built . . . the Baris near the Temple, he dwelt there most of the time . . ." (*Antiquities* 18, 91), and it is clear that he meant the refortifications (since there are earlier references to this structure). From his works it appears that the fortress served as a dwelling place for the Hasmoneans. The Hasmonean Baris was demolished and rebuilt by Herod. Only a single vestige of the Hasmonean fortress remains—a water canal hewn out of the rock below the fortress, which led to rock-cut cisterns under the present-day Temple

Mount. Another point of identification, to which many legends from the Hasmonean period have been attributed, is the Acra (Greek for "the high place" or "the fortress"), built by Antiochus III, although Josephus' words are ambiguous. This fortress was built higher than the Temple, so that it would be possible to observe whatever was taking place within the grounds. It was later reinforced by Bacchides. In 141 BCE it was conquered by Simon the Hasmonean and razed to the ground. Josephus relates that the hilltop on which the fortress stood was removed so that no one would even consider restoring the building, thus making identification today difficult.

The exact location of the Acra is unknown. Many scholars have deliberated on this problem since the beginning of archaeological exploration in Jerusalem. At first it was sought in the area of the present-day Jewish Quarter, at a site overlooking the Temple Mount. However, according to Josephus, the Acra stood at the place that lay between the Lower City (the hill of the City of David) and the Temple Mount (*Wars* 5, 4, 1; *Antiquities* 12, 252). If his account of the destruction of the fortress and the removal of the hill on which it stood is authentic, then it must be looked for in the Temple Mount area, probably in its southeastern corner. Perhaps the vestiges of an ancient building found in the vicinity of the southeastern corner of the Temple Mount are the remains of a gigantic artificial stone plinth upon which the fortress was built.

*The reconstructed room in this illustration was the largest (36 feet [11 m] long) in the* **Palatial Mansion** *and it apparently served as a* **reception hall** *for special events. It is clearly seen in the drawing of this structure.*

*This hall's decorations were unique: the walls were whitewashed, and adorned with large, marginally dressed stones; the ceiling was similarly decorated, but it also had triangular and hexagonal tiles. The style of decoration and construction, especially in this hall, is indicative of the Hellenistic influence, characteristic of the wealthy classes. The beauty of the structure ranks it with similar buildings found throughout the Roman Empire.*

## The Herodian Dynasty and the Roman Governors, 67 BCE–70 CE

Under the rule of the Herodian dynasty, Jerusalem reached the height of its prosperity as well as its optimum expansion (it was only in the nineteenth century that the city once again attained these dimensions). Archaeological findings and various descriptions from that period, mainly those by Josephus, who saw this city and knew it well, make it possible to reconstruct one of the most magnificent construction projects ever carried out in Jerusalem.

There were a number of factors that caused Herod to embellish and fortify Jerusalem, his capital city. These were the desire to increase the city's economic prosperity, as well as his own personal wealth; his passion for embellishment and his desire to immortalize himself; the need to secure his sovereignty, both internally and externally; and the need to appease the people and to keep them occupied. Because of his inclination toward the Hellenistic culture and his desire to make an impression on the Roman rulers, he set out to give Jerusalem a purely Hellenistic character. This was expressed in the building style, the magnitude and type of building he constructed (for example, a theater and a hippodrome). Herod built palaces, erected fortifications, reinforced the structures on the Temple Mount, and renovated the Temple, all with a magnificence previously unknown in Jerusalem. Vestiges of many of the buildings erected by Herod in Jerusalem still remain to this day, such as the walls of the Temple Mount, the Citadel ("Tower of David"), and more. The development of the city continued unceasingly after his death (4 BCE), and building continued up to the destruction of the Second Temple (70 CE). This was especially true during the rule of Agrippa I (41–44 CE), when there seemed to be a religious revival as evidenced in the Western Wall tunnels, where Herodian structures were demolished to make room for ritual baths and similar structures.

Herod repaired and rebuilt the First Wall, the construction of which began during the Hasmonean period. It appears that Herod also added the Second Wall, which accelerated the expansion of the city in a northerly direction, beyond the Upper City hill. One of the main fortifications reinforced by Herod in the First Wall was in the vicinity of the present-day Citadel. In this area, where he also built his palace (in the Upper City; *Wars* 5, 4, 3), he reinforced and embellished two towers (the Phasael and Mariamme towers) built in the Hasmonean era. On the site of a third tower dating to that period, he built the Hippicus Tower, known today as David's Tower. Herod also fortified the Hasmonean wall south of the Citadel—originally built on a rock for the protection of the Upper City. In the course of time, he erected his palace on an elevated section in this area. The city wall became a sort of retaining wall and in order to augment it, Herod built an adjoining anterior wall. This wall was 10 feet (3.5 m) high in some sections, and most of it later served as the basis for the Ottoman wall. Remains of these fortifications are preserved to this day. The most striking aspect of the remains of this wall is the carved rock face surrounding Mount Zion, part of which runs underneath the Gobat School and the nearby Protestant cemetery. Archaeological finds reveal that in the vicinity of Mount Zion a gate existed in the city wall, which may well be the Gate of the Essenes through which the Essenes would emerge to relieve themselves in the Hinnom Valley at a site called Bethsoa (latrine).

The remains of the wall traced in 1894 to 1897 by Bliss and Dickie, along the southern crest of Mount Zion, are evidence that the wall ran from the area where today the Protestant cemetery is situated, in the direction of the ancient Siloam Pool. At this point, the wall traversed the dam at the outlet of the pool, and then ran to the east and north along the eastern slopes of the City of David hill, passed by the Ophel and linked up with the Temple Mount wall. The location of the juncture with the Temple Mount wall was found slightly to the north of the present southeast corner of the mount, called by scholars the "Seam," where the two different styles of building are visible. Since the wall was erected when the Temple Mount was still in its earlier size, it is difficult to discern the corner juncture of the Herodian Temple Mount.

From the other side of the Hippicus Tower, the wall ran eastward in the direction of the Temple Mount. Adjacent to the tower there was a gate in the wall, which could possibly be what Josephus called the Hidden Gate (*Wars* 5, 6, 5). East of this point, two sections were found which at the time

(*above and right*) **The Temple Mount during the Second Temple period** (*plan and reconstruction*) *in which an attempt has been made to assemble all existing data about the Temple Mount from historical sources, from archaeological remains, and through comparison of buildings on the Temple Mount with similar structures in countries in the region.*

*In the center is the Temple, with its courtyards and buildings. The Temple is divided into three sections—in the east is the Women's Court with its four chambers, in the middle is the Court of Israel, and to its west is the sanctuary* (*Hekhal*), *in front of which is the altar. The area around the Temple Mount is apparently the Hasmonean boundary, to which the laws of uncleanliness and purity applied. For this reason it was separated by a low wall upon which were stone inscriptions warning that this was the entrance to a holy place. Herod extended the Temple Mount area beyond the Hasmonean structure, and built four porticoes around the new courtyard, thereby creating a structure of three porticoes and the southern portico which was of particular interest. It was here that Herod built the Royal Portico, a structure of the type that existed in other temples of that period. It is thought that it was in these three porticoes and the Royal Portico that visitors to the city during the pilgrimage festivals passed their time.*

*The Royal Portico was so called because in the time of the Second Temple it was believed to have been built by King Solomon, as it was perhaps the last visible remains of the early Temple Mount. Herod extended the Temple Mount northward and southward to accord with the elevations he had built. According to the New Testament* (*Acts 5:12*) *this was the gathering place of the early Christians of Jerusalem.*

*Below the Royal Portico, underground passages can be seen, leading from the street south of the portico to the Temple Mount. To the west of the mount were two similar underground passages connecting the Temple Mount with the Upper City. There, too, two more passageways ran above the bridges between these two areas. One was the bridge above Wilson's Arch, over which ran the aqueduct that conducted water from Solomon's Pools to the Temple. The second passageway ran above Robinson's Arch, and from there to the imposing steps that descended from the Royal Portico to the street. Further on was a stairway which led to the Upper City itself. In addition, there was a passage to the east, in the vicinity*

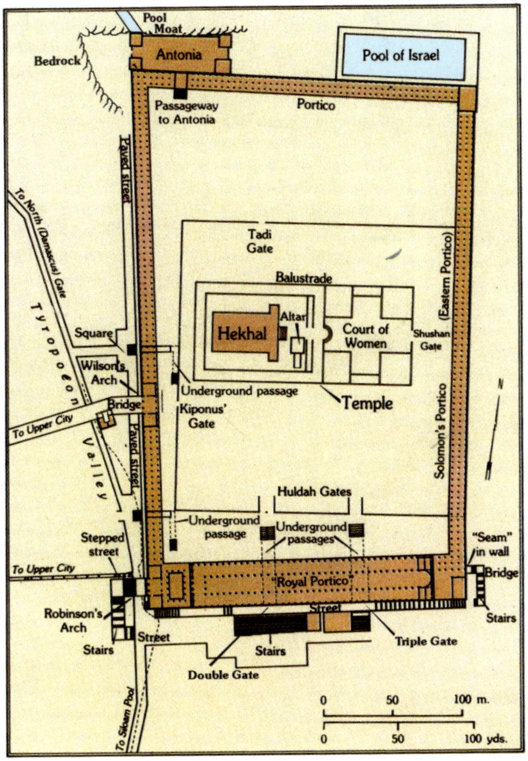


*of the southeastern corner of the mount, evidence of whose existence is provided by the stones of the archway within the eastern wall, near the "Seam." A further passageway existed in the north, leading to the Antonia fortress. Between the Antonia and the Temple Mount was a gate, but no remains of it have been found in the Temple Mount area.*

*The plan shows the network of streets outside the Temple Mount, whose existence has been attested by archaeological excavations. A beautifully paved street has been uncovered, running along the length of the western Temple Mount wall, and recently sections of it were found in the northwestern section of the mount. Its breadth was not uniform throughout, since a square was built (for architectural purposes) in front of each underground gate. A street ran along the Tyropoeon Valley to the present-day Damascus Gate in the north and to the Siloam Pool area in the south. From this network of streets, other streets ran to the west. One street branched off from the main street in an easterly direction, ran along the southern wall of the Temple Mount, and at certain places steps were built, as dictated by the topography of that particular section of the hill. Two sets of stairs led to this street from the City of David in the south and then to the Temple Mount through the two southern gates called today the Double and Triple Gates.*

*In the vicinity of the western street, Herodian period structures were discovered by Charles Warren, one of which he called the Hall of the Freemasons. Apparently these were important public buildings. Another building was found north of Robinson's Arch facing the paved road adjacent to the western wall of the Temple Mount.*

*In the tractate* Middoth *of the Mishnah, it is stated that the early Temple Mount (apparently from the third century* BCE*) had five gates: the two Huldah Gates in the south, Kiponus' Gate in the west, the Tadi Gate in the north, and the Shushan Gate in the east. In the course of extending the Temple Mount, Herod erected two gates in the south, four in the west, and an unknown number in the north. In the eastern side, in the area where Herod did not make any changes, apparently only one gate was left. The diagram points up the relationship between the proportions of the Temple and the entire Temple Mount, and for this reason the Temple has not been portrayed in detail.*

*(below) Two fragments of an* **inscription** *found near the steps leading to the southern gates of the Temple Mount. Allusions in contemporary historical sources lead us to believe that these imposing steps also served as a place of assembly. Part of the Hebrew word* zekenim *(elders) visible in the inscription, may refer to the elders of the Sanhedrin who assembled at the site. "Rabban Gamaliel and the elders would stand upon the steps of the Temple Mount"* (Tosephta, Sanhedrin 2, 2).

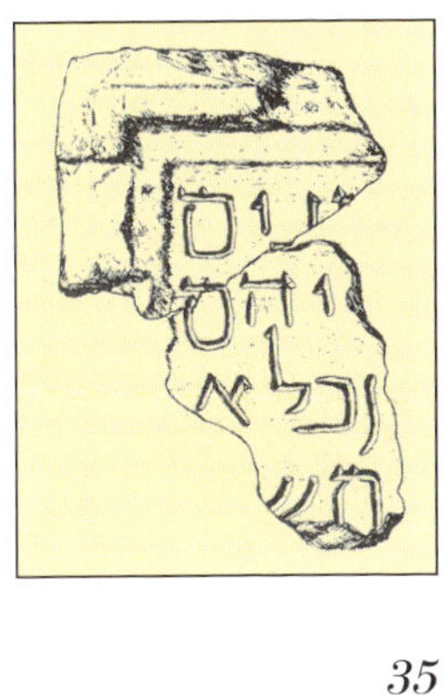

were considered to be the First Wall. One of them was near the present-day Franciscan Information Center and the other underneath the Lutheran hostel. Wilson unearthed two towers in the second section of the wall 59 feet (18 m) distant from each other. This discovery was in keeping with the information we have about the abundance of towers in the First Wall. However, the date of these towers is not clear, and may have been in the Middle Ages. The finds which are definitely connected with the northern course of the First Wall were discovered in the Jewish Quarter. These included remains of a gate and tower built of meticulously carved stones. According to Josephus, the wall continued in the direction of the Xystos, reached the Council Building, and continued toward the western portico of the Temple Mount. The Xystos and the Council Building were undoubtedly situated within the area of the present-day Jewish Quarter, but they have not been uncovered in archaeological digs, and thus it is difficult to identify them exactly.

Apparently the First Wall did not reach the western portico of the Temple Mount, but continued in the direction of a tower which we consider to have been located on the edge of the eastern ridge of the Upper City. It is difficult to believe that the wall ended here without a tower, since at the point where the wall reached the slope descending toward the Tyropoeon, there was a bridge, which carried the water conduit leading to the Temple Mount (a number of vaults of the bridge have been unearthed, the most famous being Wilson's Arch, attached to the Western Wall of the Temple Mount), and to its west two vaults of the Herodian bridge, discovered in 2006. It can be assumed that a tower was situated at this point, with the purpose of defending the end of the wall and the bridge (it is difficult to conjecture that the wall passed over the bridge). According to Josephus (*Wars* 2, 16, 3) the bridge linked the Temple Mount with the Xystos near the Hasmonean palace. The steep slope covering the entire Western Hill at the side of the escarpment, descending in the direction of the Tyropoeon Valley (today a section of this slope can be discerned opposite the Western Wall square), provided a natural line of defense against the Roman attacks from the Temple Mount area, in the direction of the Upper City (as will be seen below).

As Jerusalem continued to expand northward, a new wall was built, which Josephus calls the Second Wall. It would seem that this wall was built during Herod's rule, since it is not mentioned earlier, nor is reference to it found in the descriptions of the capture of Jerusalem, which state that only one wall surrounded the city (*Wars* 1, 17, 8–9; 18, 2). The remains of the wall, and Josephus' statement that it was connected with the Antonia fortress built by Herod, support the assumption that the wall was built in his time. An important archaeological find possibly connected with the Second Wall is the section of the wall built from Herodian-style cut stone, discovered in the excavations carried out at the Damascus Gate in the 1930s (these remains are today covered over). The position of the wall leads to the conclusion that it adjoined the tower situated west of the gate in the wall. Another suggestion is that these remains are actually the foundation of the Roman tower that flanks the gate. Apart from these remains, no further sections of this wall have been found, only a fleeting mention of which is made by Josephus. (Archaeological finds made in the grounds of the Church of the Redeemer and the Russian Hospice near the Church of the Holy Sepulcher, were for years considered to be part of the Second Wall, but today it is recognized that the finds, which date from the Roman period, have no connection whatsoever to this wall.)

The lack of data, which prevents the exact demarcation of the course of the Second Wall, has led to numerous speculations. We will attempt to reconstruct the course of the wall (partly according to the sites still extant), based on descriptions in Josephus' writings and the few remains discovered, and taking into consideration the topographical structure of the area. The wall began at the Antonia fortress, continued to the north along the Beth Zetha incline to the western edge of Herod's Gate; from here it continued along the present-day northern wall up to Damascus Gate. In this area the course of the wall ran alongside the moat (still visible) which was apparently excavated in the Middle Ages; from the Damascus Gate it ran south to the Muristan area, along Habad Street, ed-Dabagha (Dyers' Market) Street and the Christians' Street down to the point where it meets David Street. The Gennath (Garden) Gate was situated nearby, but it has not yet been identified. However, it can be assumed that it was situated near the point where the Second Wall encountered the First Wall. The description

*(left) The term* **"Seam"** *is used to describe a point in the eastern Temple Mount wall, 105 feet (32 m) north of the southwest corner of the city wall, where two styles of dressed stones are evident. These are clearly visible in the photograph. To the north (right) of this line is the Temple Mount wall, built from coarse, marginally dressed stones, and to the south (left) are finely hewn stones, with embossed smooth faces, and delicate margins along the edges, in the typical Herodian style.*

*Scholars are of the opinion that the northern part of this section of the wall is the eastern side of the southeastern corner of the Temple Mount wall from the Hasmonean period. Another assumption is that these are the remains of the Acra fortress from the Hellenistic period. The style in which the stones were cut in the section south of the "Seam," and the style of building in this section, are characteristic of the Herodian period. It is now generally accepted that this section of the wall is an extension of the Temple Mount wall built by Herod when he extended the area of the Hasmonean Temple Mount toward the north, west, and south. This has strengthened the conclusion that the section north of the "Seam" is part of the pre-Herodian Temple Mount wall. This assumption is based on the fact that the stone cutting and the construction at this point were done in a style similar to that of third- and second-century* BCE *buildings found at other sites in the Mediterranean region.*

*In the area south of the "Seam," projections (of about 40 square cm) remaining in the wall can be discerned. These stones were used to carry the large stones to their destination, but once the building operation was completed, these stones were not cut as was customarily done. Also visible is part of a large archway, which is evidence of the existence of a bridge that was used by persons leaving through the two gates, situated above the archway. These gates were smaller than the other gates of the Temple Mount, as indicated by their remains, and it seems that they were used by a small number of people. On the lower courses of this section of the wall, lying on bedrock, remains of inscriptions in ancient Hebrew were found by Warren, who sunk one of his shafts at this point. In these inscriptions, the letter* kof *recurs. This may indicate the use of the word* kadosh *(holy) by the builders of this colossal wall.*

*(below)* **Pilgrimages** *to the Temple in Jerusalem on the three pilgrimage festivals and during the rest of the year express the centrality of the city in the Second Temple period. The* halakha *determined that the meal offerings, priestly tithes, and the sacrifices were to be from the finest agricultural produce brought from every place in the land where Jews lived. The sources list the settlements where the produce was the choicest and fit to be brought to the Temple (tractate* Minhot *88, 1).*

*The* **entrance ban inscription** *was one of the inscriptions in Greek or Latin placed in the wall enclosing the sanctified area of the Temple Mount intended to warn outsiders against entering the area. The Greek inscription presented here has been reconstructed according to an inscription found in 1871 near the "Dark Gate" (Bab el-Atm) on the Temple Mount. The section in the photograph is from another inscription discovered in the vicinity of the Lions' Gate in 1935. The text in both inscriptions is legible, stating: "Foreigner do not enter within the grille and the partition surrounding the Temple. He who is caught will have only himself to blame for his death."*

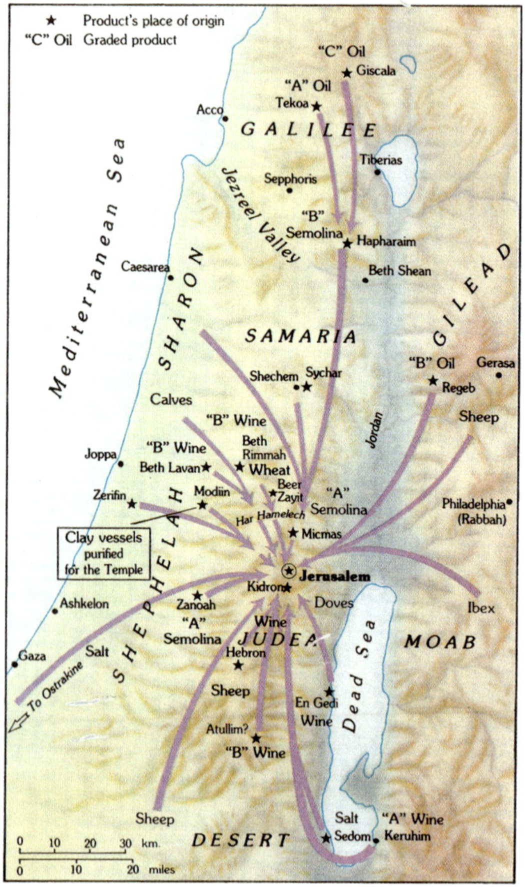

*(right)* **Stone of the Trumpeting Place**. *The excavations of the southern wall revealed streets bordering the Temple Mount wall running from the north and the west. At the time of the destruction of the city in 70 CE, gigantic blocks of stone, from which the walls of the Temple Mount were constructed, toppled onto these streets. In the vicinity of the southwestern corner of the mount, a huge stone was found on which was inscribed:*

**"Leveit hatekiya lehav. . ."** *(to the Trumpeting Place to sepa[rate] . . .) (Mishnah,* Sukkah *5:5). The phrase probably ended in the word* lehavdil *(to separate). Josephus* (Wars *4: 577) writes that the Sabbath was ushered from above the holy enclosure, and thus he may have been referring to the southwestern corner of the wall where the stone block was situated before the wall was demolished.*

*This* **reconstruction of the southwest corner of the Temple Mount** *depicts the magnificence of the building on the Temple Mount after the end of Herod's construction projects.*

*This section clearly shows the embellished western gate leading to the Royal Portico. This portico constituted the southern area of the Temple Mount, from which steps descended to the Tyropoeon Valley below. All that remains are the bases of the piers which supported the stairway as well as the springers of the upper arch called* **Robinson's Arch.** *From the time Charles Warren carried out his excavations at this location, it was obvious that this was not a bridge, but the scholarly literature continued to claim that a bridge existed there. Excavations carried out by B. Mazar in the 1970s proved conclusively that the structure portrayed here actually existed in the manner illustrated. The protruding attached pillars, which decorated the Temple Mount walls, have been preserved only at its northwestern corner. They were discovered and first described by Conder while carrying out the British-sponsored survey in Palestine.*

*The extremity of the wall and its cornerstones are restored here in accordance with the "Stone of the Trumpeting Place" found in the street abutting the wall. The assumed location of the stone, and the point where the trumpeter stood, are depicted in the illustration (opposite) by a figure blowing a trumpet at the corner of the wall.*

*At the foot of the arch, a network of streets in this section of the city can be seen. Josephus describes the stairways and the street leading from them to the west in his* Antiquities (15, 11, 5).

*(right) An attempt to reconstruct* **Barclay's Gate** *(cross section) based on archaeological findings and the writings of Josephus. Over the years the original structural form of this gate has changed, but a section of it is still extant and is used as a mosque and as a water cistern on the Temple Mount. The original lintel and western opening can be seen in the women's section of the Western Wall prayer area.*

*The reconstruction shows the western stairway of the passage ascending to the Temple Mount.*

*The cross section also shows the reconstruction of the western portico, based on Josephus' account* (Wars *5, 5, 2). The reconstruction of the parapet is based on the discovery of the "Stone of the Trumpeting Place," as well as other archaeological finds. At the bottom of the mount, the riverbed of the Tyropoeon Valley can be seen, running along the foot of the western wall of the early Temple Mount, and underneath the Herodian Temple Mount. A drainage canal has been found attached to the western wall of the mount. The theory that the pre-Herodian Temple Mount wall was situated in the vicinity is based on the assumption that the Tyropoeon Valley constituted the western boundary of the Temple Mount in the Hasmonean period, and it was Herod who extended the Temple Mount westward, beyond the valley. To this end he also built a new drainage network which can be seen on the western slope of the Tyropoeon Valley.*

*A street ran along the length of the western side of the Temple Mount, and this appears in the cross section diagram as the upper street. A number of entrances opened onto this street, and these were apparently used as shops which are depicted in the diagram by an archway below the street.*

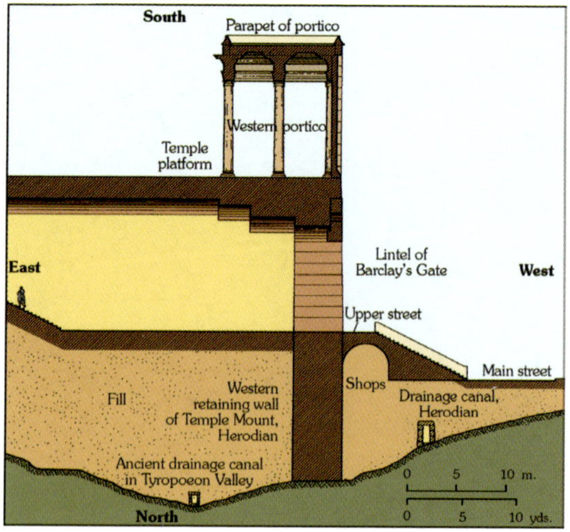

*(left and above) Remains of* **Robinson's Arch** *found in the Temple Mount wall, in the southern section of the Western Wall. The arch is named after the explorer Edward Robinson, who first described it in a work published in 1838. All that remains of the arch, which was about 44 feet (13.5 m) wide, are the springers protruding from the Temple Mount wall and the retaining stone course below it which also protrudes from the wall.*

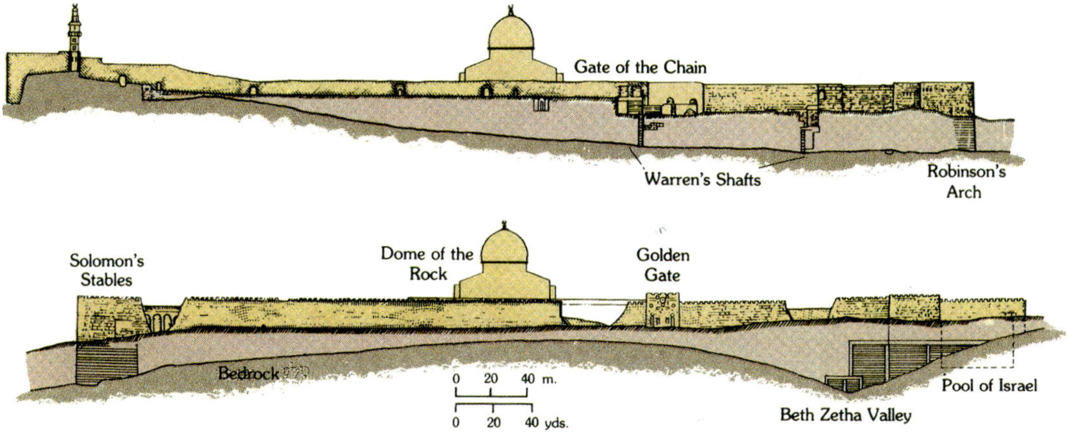


*Views of* **the western (top) and eastern walls of the Temple Mount** *which appeared in Charles Warren's books and atlas in which he published the summation of his exploration of Jerusalem during the years 1867 to 1870. Looking across the Temple Mount wall from the west (the upper illustration) evidence can be seen of the quarrying carried out in the Herodian period in the natural bedrock in the northwestern corner of the Temple Mount required for the construction of the Antonia fortress. The Bani Ghawanima minaret today stands in the center of the elevated rocky plateau upon which the Antonia stood.*

*From the eastern view of the Temple Mount wall (lower illustration) the ancient Beth Zetha Valley and the southeastern corner of the Temple Mount built upon the bedrock are easily visible. At this point, Warren dug down and reached the natural rock. It was here that he found the Hebrew letter* kof *painted on the lowest course of the Temple Mount wall. It would seem that this was the first letter of the word* kadosh *(holy).*

*(above) "***Theodotus***, son of Vettenos, priest and head of the synagogue, son of the head of the synagogue, who was also the son of the head of the synagogue, built the synagogue for the reading of the Law and for the study of the precepts, as well as the hospice and the chambers and the bathing establishment, for lodging those who need them, from abroad; it (the synagogue) was founded by his ancestors and the elders and Simonides."*

*This* **inscription** *was written in Greek and the style of its characters dates it to the time of Herod. This is evidence that synagogues existed in Jerusalem at the time when the Temple was still standing.*

*The inscription was found in a large cistern during the excavations carried out by R. Weill in 1913–1914. The cistern contained many architectural remains of a nearby building that had been demolished. It appears that the structure was of outstanding splendor, as evidenced by the decorated pillars and stone blocks found in the cistern. The building was probably demolished at the time of the destruction of the Second Temple, and its remains cast into the cistern, perhaps in the hope that it would someday be rebuilt.*

of Jesus' Garden Tomb (John 19:41) leads us to assume that the area was rich in gardens, and this was the source of the name of the gate. A gate found in the First Wall during the Jewish Quarter excavations leads to the conjecture that the line of the wall may have been shorter, running through the markets in the heart of the city and making a direct turn toward the Antonia fortress.

The Second Wall was shorter than the First and the Third: according to Josephus it had fourteen towers, as compared with sixty in the First Wall and ninety in the Third Wall. In the area added to the inside of the wall, dwellings and public storehouses were built. The wall ran around the middle section of the Tyropoeon Valley, from which it was possible to enter the Temple Mount (through Warren's Gate), as well as the Antonia fortress.

Scholars are convinced that the existence of the Second Temple period tombs in the Church of the Holy Sepulcher upholds the theory that in the first century CE the church area lay outside the city walls and served as a burial ground. Thus it cannot be presumed that it came within the area of the Second Wall, which served as the city wall in the time of Jesus.

The Third Wall is described in detail by Josephus (*Wars* 5, 4, 2). According to his account, it was Agrippa I who planned it and began its construction, but was forced to cease building at the order of the Romans. It was completed by the Zealots in 41–44 and again in 67–69, prior to the siege of Jerusalem.

According to Josephus, the wall ran from the Hippicus Tower to Psephinus' Tower in the west of the city, passed opposite the Tomb of Queen Helene and the Royal Cave, bypassed the Fuller's Monument, touched the Old Wall of the Temple Mount and descended to the Kidron Valley. We still do not know how and where it linked up with the ancient walls, since its eastern and western sections have still not been found, despite the numerous excavations carried out along the course it was presumed to have followed. Perhaps the great dam built by Herod to block up the Beth Zetha Valley, thus creating the Pool of Israel just north of the Temple Mount, served as the base for the Third Wall at the connecting point with the Temple Mount wall.

Remnants of the northern section of the Third Wall have been preserved to this day. Already in the nineteenth century remains had been found in the north of the city (to the east and west of the present-day Damascus Road, near the American Consulate in the eastern part of the city). The sections found were about 2,950 feet (900 m) long, and ran in an east-west direction. From the numerous archaeological finds made along the length of the wall between 1925 and 1974 (especially by E. L. Sukenik and L. A. Mayer), it has become apparent that these are sections of the wall demolished at the time of the destruction of Jerusalem in 70 CE. Their discovery raised disputes among scholars concerning the nature of the wall. Some scholars even suggested identifying it as a siege wall dating from the Bar Kokhba revolt. However, excavations held at the site in the 1980s confirmed its date to the Second Temple period.

In the area between the present-day Old City wall and the Third Wall, hardly any remains of Second Temple period buildings have been found. This fact shows that little construction work was carried out in the new section of the city (the Bezetha quarter, or the New City as Josephus called it), until about the time of the destruction of Jerusalem.

The Temple and the Temple Mount were the focal point of religious, spiritual, and political life during the Second Temple period. The archaeological data reveal a most impressive picture of the development of the Temple Mount at this time, which reached its climax during Herod's reign.

The topography of the Temple Mount was changed radically by Herod. He quarried into and leveled the hill northwest of the mount, and thus expanded the Temple compound and its sanctified area. He built a broad terrace encompassing the mount—to the north, south, and west—upon which porticoes were later erected. It would seem that from the outset the Temple Mount was built more or less in the form of a square, and according to the Mishnah its dimensions were 500×500 cubits (approximately 740×740 feet [225×225 m]). The traditionally accepted description of the shape and size of the Temple Mount is quite ancient, possibly earlier than the Hasmonean period. The Book of Ezekiel already describes it as being square (45:2). The key to understanding the changes that were brought about lies in the "Seam" in the eastern wall (105 feet [32 m] north of the southeastern corner of the Temple Mount). As mentioned earlier, the two styles of construc-

*The description of the* **Antonia Fortress** *in Josephus' writings* (Wars 5, 8)*, and the descriptions of the Birah* (Baris) *in earlier sources, created the impression that the Antonia was a magnificent edifice. The various reconstructions made in the past showed that it included a large stone-paved central courtyard. However, today it is clear that the Lithostrotos, the paved area that we see today upon which, according to Christian tradition, the trial of Jesus took place* (Mark 15:17; John 19:13)*, was not part of the fortress, but is to be found in the moat to the north of it. Thus, the Antonia, with its four towers, apparently stood on the rocky surface, whose dimensions were only 148×394 feet (45×120 m), and was protected by moats surrounding it. In the photo, behind the trees, the rocky cliff is seen, on which stood the Antonia, and above it the remains of the building that was constructed over the early fortress in the Mamluk period. In the Ottoman period the site served as the residence of the Sultan's envoy in Jerusalem.*

*A reconstruction of the* **Herodian Citadel** *against the background of the present-day Citadel (the Herodian sections are shaded). When Herod ascended the throne (in 37* BCE*) he reinforced the section of the First Wall which included the three towers first built by the Hasmoneans. In parts of this section Herod thickened the Hasmonean wall. He also enlarged the central tower by covering its walls, and rebuilt the southern tower extending its height. In place of the northern Hasmonean tower, Herod erected the tower now known as "David's Tower" (at the left of the illustration).*

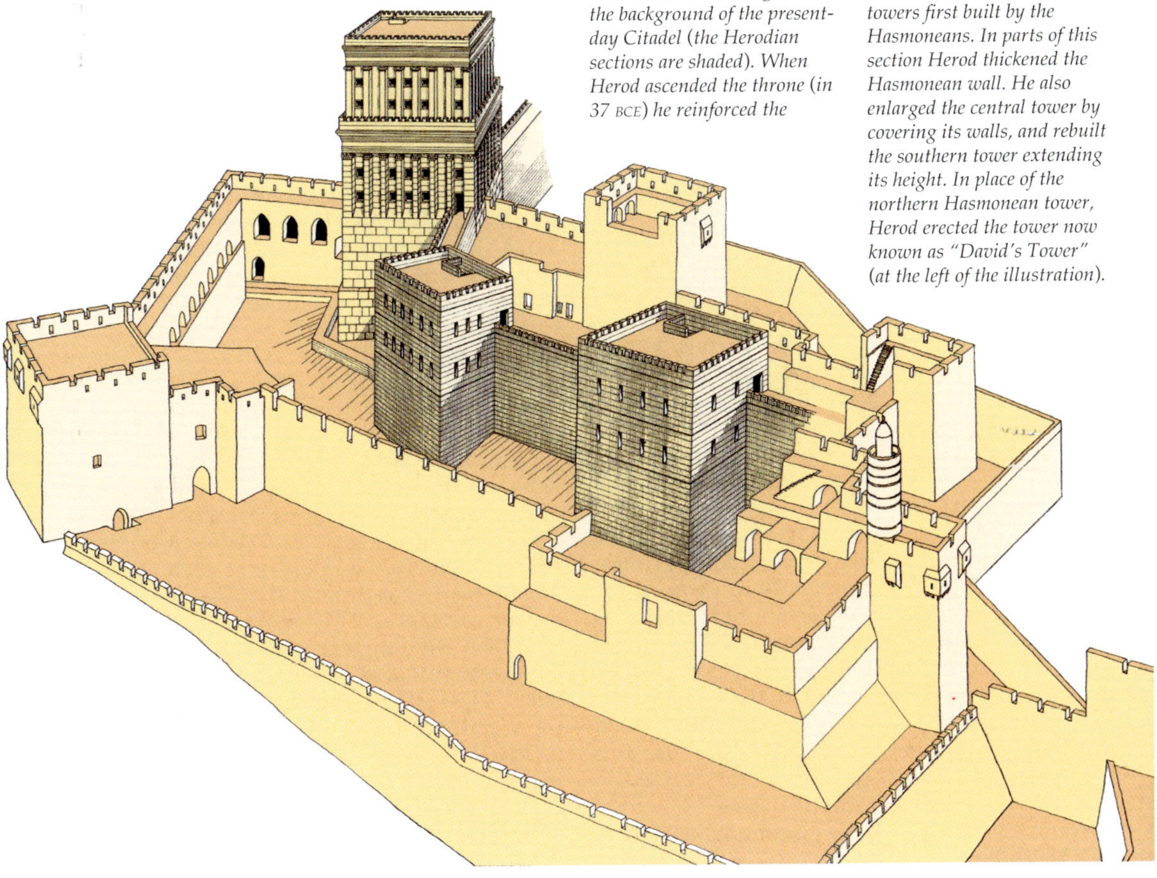

tion merged at this juncture. The northern section was typical of the style found at other Hellenistic sites; the style of the southern section was typically Herodian. It may well be that the "Seam" was the point where the Herodian construction merged with the earlier structure. However, this explanation is not accepted by many scholars, and there are those who believe that the "Seam" was the meeting point between the Acra—the fortress built by the Seleucids in Jerusalem—and the expansion carried out during Herod's rule.

In Herod's time the custom of erecting temples for Caesarean worship was already popular. Temples of this type, called Caesareum (plural Caesarea), were generally large compounds in the center of which was the temple surrounded by a portico. Similar Caesarea have been found in several cities in the Orient, such as Antioch, Tadmor, Alexandria, and Cyrene. The Temple Mount compound and the Temple were built in the form of a Caesareum, and was inspired too by the pre-Herodian structure that Herod saw there.

Herod began to build the Temple in the eighteenth year of his reign (apparently 19 BCE), and according to Josephus the construction work continued for a further nine years, eight of which were devoted to erecting the portico and the compound, while the building of the sanctuary itself took one year and five months (*Antiquities* 15, 420–421). The New Testament states that the construction took forty-six years (John 2:20). Apparently the project did take a considerable length of time, as Josephus notes that it was during the time of the governor Albinus (62–64 CE) that the building was completed (*Antiquities* 20, 209). Archaeological results reveal that despite all this, the work on the Temple Mount had never been finished.

The major effort and time were devoted to the construction of the porticoes, the main architectural elements of the Temple Mount. One of the porticoes, described in full detail by Josephus, is the Royal Portico (the basilica) at the southern end of the compound (*Antiquities* 15, 411–420). This portico served as a commercial center for the sale of ritual articles, and may well be that called the "shops" in other sources. Perhaps also this was the site to which the seat of the Sanhedrin was moved shortly before the destruction of the Second Temple (Babylonian Talmud, *Shabbat* 16, 71). Herod linked the Royal Portico with the Upper City by a street, stairs, and an arch—today known as Robinson's Arch.

With the extension of the Temple Mount area, the need arose to distinguish between the sanctified area—the ancient part—and the new, extended area to which the laws of sanctity did not apply. To this end a low wall was built, which delineated the sanctified area on the Temple Mount compound. Stone inscriptions in Greek and Latin were placed on this partition, warning Gentiles not to cross beyond this point so as not to enter the sanctified section of the Temple Mount (*Wars* 5, 5, 2). The importance of the partition wall, which precisely delineated the sanctified section, is still of the utmost importance regarding the halakhic prohibition of Jews entering the Temple Mount.

The Antonia fortress played a vital role in the defense of Jerusalem in the time of Herod. In order to maintain control over the Temple and to defend the Temple Mount at its most vulnerable point, the northwestern corner, Herod turned the Baris (Birah in Nehemiah's time) situated there into a large fortress which he called the Antonia, in honor of Marc Antony. The Antonia was apparently erected in order to replace and extend the ancient Baris, which was demolished when Herod extended the Temple Mount northward. The Baris served, among other things, as a dwelling place for the rulers and kings of the Hasmonean dynasty. No vestiges of this earlier fortress have remained. This phenomenon—demolishing earlier structures to make way for new ones—is familiar from other sites where Herod built outside Jerusalem.

The Antonia was built on an elevated rocky plateau (148×394 feet [45×120 m]), cut off on all sides by moats dug to the north and west, by a natural steep incline descending to the east, and by the leveling of the Temple Mount to the south. A tower was placed at each corner and one of them—the Straton Tower at the southwest corner—was especially well fortified. The extent to which the stone was excavated leads us to believe that it was of particularly broad dimensions, especially to the north (the tower reached the vicinity of the present-day Bani Ghawanima minaret). Josephus describes the Antonia as having bathhouses, courtyards, porticoes, and numerous rooms. Apart from this portrayal, there is no other evidence available of the interior of the fortress, especially because of the numerous (*below*) *Reconstruction of the* **Double Gate** *as it existed in Herod's time. From its two openings, divided by an elongated pier, two passages lead to the Temple Mount separated by a series of columns as a continuation of the pier. The ceilings of the passageways had decorated domes. The original decorations from the Herodian period have remained on three of them, partly covered with stucco in the style prevalent in Jerusalem at that time. This style can be seen in decorations in burial caves and sarcophagi dating to this penod. These included grapevines, clusters of grapes, rosettas and other adornments.*

*According to the Mishnah* (Middoth 1) *there were two gates—the Huldah Gates—in the southern wall of the pre-Herodian Temple Mount. When Herod extended the Temple Mount toward the south, he also built two gates in the new southern wall. The eastern one is called the Triple Gate, and the western, the Double Gate, and there is no evidence for these to have also been called the "Huldah Gates." Passageways led from them directly to the interior of the Temple Mount.*

*Remains of these two gates can be seen in the southern wall of the Temple Mount some 558 feet (170 m) distant from its eastern extremity.*

**Decorated frame of the Triple Gate** *hewn out of the stone slab surrounding the gate. The gate has remained in its original form from the Herodian era, and the decoration is the only vestige found so far of adornments of the Temple Mount gates from that period. Near the gate can be seen names of Jewish pilgrims carved in the stone while visiting the site, probably dating to the end of the Arab period.*

*The northwestern corner of the Temple Mount had always been its most vulnerable point because of the topography of the land lying to the north—a hill higher than the mount itself, to the north of which was the Antonia Ridge. Evidence exists that in the biblical era a fortress was situated at this corner, for the purpose of protecting the Temple Mount. At the end of the First Temple penod, the Hananel Tower was built on this site, and during the Hasmonean period the Baris stood there.*

*However, Herod radically changed the face of the hill. Parts were removed to bring it to the level of the Temple Mount (the lower section to the south was filled in with earth). On its north and west sides a series of moats were dug, thus forming a rock platform upon which the* **Antonia Fortress** *was built, named after Herod's patron, the military commander Marc Antony. This rock platform is the only remnant of the stronghold. The photo shows the rocky areas exposed in the course of quarrying at the foot of the hill upon which the Antonia stood.*

structures built on the Antonia Ridge during the Mamluk period. Stairs led down from the Antonia to the porticoes which encircled the Temple Mount (*Wars* 5, 5, 8). A number of concealed passages connected the fortress to the Temple Mount, and Josephus mentions one of them (*Antiquities* 15, 424).

In Herod's time, the Upper City was a residential quarter for the Hellenized wealthy, and Herod's palace, as well as Hasmonean and other palaces were constructed within its confines. Herod's palace, the most magnificent of them, was described in superlatives by Josephus, especially because of its gardens, porticoes, and fountains. It was divided into two sections: the Caesareon, after Augustus Caesar, and the Agrippeon, after the Roman military leader Vipsanius Agrippa. In the past it was assumed that the fortress and its three towers—Hippicus, Mariamme, and Phasael—seemed to protect the palace, but from the excavations it became apparent that these, if indeed these are the towers discovered in the excavations of the fortress, were part of the series of sixty towers in the Hasmonean wall (the First Wall). The palace itself was a virtual fortress because of the walls surrounding it. It is possible that it also served as the residence of Roman governors such as Pontius Pilate. According to the New Testament (John 19:13), Pontius Pilate sat in judgment over Jesus at the Lithostrotos (a place paved with stone) which is Gabbatha. This site may also be within the confines of Herod's palace.

In the area between Herod's palace and the section of the wall where the three towers stood, was the residential area. This included one street built up on both sides. The palace and residential quarter were built on an elevated plateau, which rested on retaining walls remaining from the Hasmonean period. These walls were found

*Reconstruction of the* **Siloam Pool** *in the Second Temple period based mainly on excavations carried out at the site by Bliss and Dickie from 1894 to 1897 and by Reich and Shukron in the 1990s. In the excavations the tower complex (to the right of the illustration) has been uncovered once again, and also the Siloam Pool and the streets leading to it from the city.*

*During the First Temple period the pool received its supply of water from Hezekiah's Tunnel. This tunnel continued to supply the pool during the Second Temple period and later. In the riverbed a 66 foot (20 m) wide dam was built, reinforced by a series of attached pillars erected on the extended base. These pillars were uncovered in the excavation carried out by Bliss and Dickie, when they descended a series of tunnels at various points of the structure. There are those who question the accuracy of the reconstruction based on the findings presented here. The dam's width has only been estimated, and it is possible that the dimensions of the structure as it is shown in this illustration are based on a combination of finds from the Second Temple period as well as the First Temple period, since such a dam existed during the earlier period as well. The city wall passed over the dam when it crossed the valley between the City of David (right) and Mount Zion (left), which was part of the city when the dam was built. At the foot of Mount Zion, a street was discovered paved with large stone slabs. The street led to a postern in the wall, which can also be seen in the illustration. This postern was apparently utilized again in the fifth century, when the Empress Eudocia reconstructed the southern city wall, and continued in use until the destruction of the wall in the eleventh century.*

*The Siloam Pool is situated on the site of today's Birket el-Hamra.*

in the excavations carried out in the Citadel and in the present-day Armenian Garden—the only remains of this magnificent palace.

During this period there was also the Hasmonean palace, into which the Hasmoneans moved after leaving the Baris (*Antiquities* 15, 11, 410). Agrippa I and Agrippa II also lived in this palace. It was apparently situated on the eastern slope of the Upper City, at a point overlooking the Temple Mount. Finds from archaeological excavations carried out in the Jewish Quarter reveal that in the eastern section of the Upper City there was a large concentration of wealthy mansions. Today, there are remains of the Palatial Mansion and the Burnt House, but no vestige of the Hasmonean palace has yet been uncovered. It is almost certain that the architectural style of the Hasmonean palace was similar to that of these mansions..

A further concentration of palaces known from historical sources, was found on the hill of the City of David, which continued to serve as an important part of the city's administrative complex. These were the palaces of the Adiabene royal family: the palace of Queen Helene (*Wars* 5, 6, 1; 6, 6, 3); the palace of the House of Monobaz (*Wars* 5, 6, 1); and the palaces affiliated with the Graphte family (*Wars* 4, 9, 11). These palaces mentioned by Josephus have not been discovered by the archaeologists, and thus their location cannot be determined except in the most general terms. Apart from the magnificent palaces characteristic of Jerusalem under Herod's rule, other sites were referred to in historical sources. The exact location is not known (and therefore not marked in our map) of the monument to Alexander in the northeast of the city, the monument to Jonathan in the northwest, and the above-mentioned palaces of the Adiabene family. Scholars believe that a hippodrome mentioned a number of times by Josephus (*Antiquities* 17, 255; *Wars* 2, 3, 1) was situated south of the Temple Mount. Archaeological finds have not provided evidence of this, nor have they proved the assumption incorrect.

The provision of water has always been a major problem in Jerusalem. In Herod's time tremendous efforts were made to exploit to the full the many water resources available. The Gihon Spring was one of the most important of these sources. Until recently scholars believed that the spring was blocked up during the time of Hezekiah's rule, and its waters ran into the Siloam Pool. However, recent archaeological excavations reveal that the Gihon Spring also served as a source of water for the City of David hill area in Herodian times..

**Hasmonean subterranean canal** *through which water was brought to the cisterns underneath the Baris fortress, the seat of the Hasmonean rulers. During the course of extensions to the Temple Mount, the canal was severed at various points and thus was rendered useless. The canal was discovered in October 1867 by Charles Warren, but was blocked up in 1870 and rediscovered on March 16, 1987, by Israeli explorers. This is undoubtedly one of the most exciting vestiges of Jerusalem's past. The site is open to the public.*

There were also many pools in Jerusalem. The Siloam Pool, whose waters derived from the Gihon Spring, supplied water mainly to the City of David and its vicinity. When describing the First Wall, Josephus relates to another pool in this area, which he calls Solomon's Pool. Until recently it was thought that this was an error and that Solomon's Pool was actually the Siloam Pool.

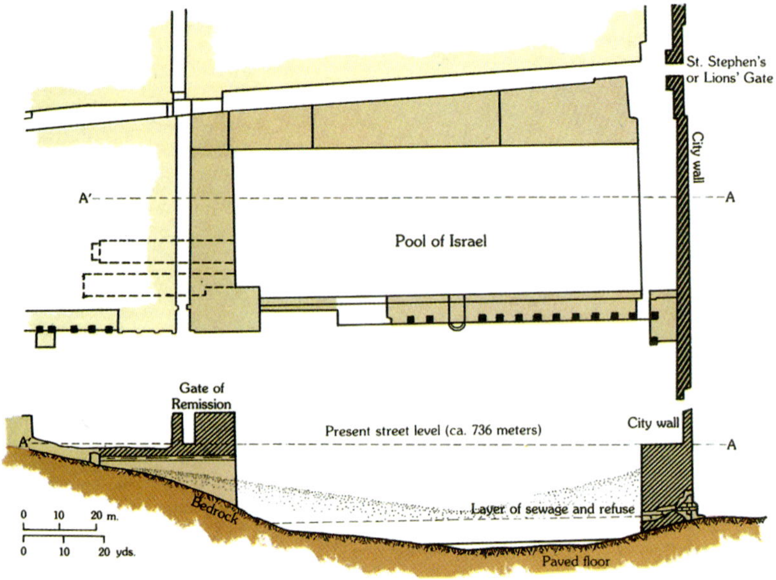


*(right) Prior to the Herodian period the Temple Mount was bounded by a network of streams to the west, north, and east. When Herod extended the Temple Mount compound, he stopped up the course of the Beth Zetha Valley to the north, and the course of the Tyropoeon Valley to the west. He also set up dams along their course to collect the water.*

*In the northern part of the* **Beth Zetha Valley**, *dams and pools were constructed already in the First Temple period, and in the early Second Temple era the Sheep's Pools were built in its riverbed. In the southern part of the valley, which was spanned by the extended Temple Mount wall, a dam was constructed, near the northeastern corner of the mount. This dam formed the* **Pool of Israel**, *which was the largest of the pools in Jerusalem. It was 361 feet (110 m) long, 131 feet (40 m) wide, and 98 feet (30 m) deep. In years when there was abundant rainfall the pool was filled with 120,000 cubic meters of water.*

*The pool's huge dimensions made a deep impression on visitors to the city throughout the ages and many of them described it in detail. In the nineteenth century, it was the subject of paintings by many artists. In 1934 the Jerusalem municipality drained this pool and sealed it because it had become a health hazard. A car park is now built over it.*

*(left) The* **Siloam Pool from the Second Temple period**. *So far only the northern part of this pool has been excavated. The pool was first installed in the Hasmonean period when it was plastered. It underwent improvements in the Herodian period when the existing steps were replaced by a stone staircase (seen in the photograph). Its discovery changed the course of pilgrim visits in the city, for the Siloam Pool marks the traditional site where Jesus performed his miracle of curing the blind man. Before then, pilgrims were accustomed to visit the site of "Siloam" identified by the Empress Eudocia in the fifth century.*

However, a chance discovery revealed remains of a large pool in the riverbed of the Kidron Valley, north of the southernmost point of the City of David. This was apparently the pool Josephus was referring to.

Another pool, the Towers' Pool, was identified with what is known as Hezekiah's Pool. This identification is generally accepted, as the only reference to it is found in Josephus (*Wars* 5, 11, 4). He states that the Romans set up a siege ramp at the site called the Towers' Pool, and at a distance of thirty cubits the Roman legions set up another ramp in the vicinity of the monument to the High Priest. Elsewhere, he states that the monument to John (the High Priest) was a siege-tower opposite the Upper City (*Wars* 5, 9, 2). This pool under-

*This schematic diagram of a family* **burial cave** *is of the type found in many necropolises in Second Temple period Jerusalem. The cemeteries which surrounded the city on all sides extended during that period from present-day Romema to French Hill in the north, to Ramat Rahel in the south, from the Mount Scopus-Mount of Olives ridge in the east, and up to Giv'at Ram in the west. Wars, chaos, and destruction which the city underwent passed over the "City of the Dead" which surrounded it.*

*After the Six-Day War of 1967, intensive construction work took place around the city, in the course of which many Second Temple burial caves were discovered. These caves revealed names and titles of persons buried there, inscriptions and ossuaries.*

*The diagram shows the forecourt hewn into the rock (in the upper section), and beyond it the entrance to the burial cave, through a narrow opening blocked by a burial stone. In the center of the burial chamber was a wide pit, in which persons carrying out the burial could stand up erect. The smaller pit to the lower left of the chamber served for the placing of bones of persons buried there previously. (In the Second Temple period the remains of the dead were collected several years after they were first buried, and preserved in ossuaries, thus making room for others in the family burial cave.) At the sides of the chambers niches can be seen where the ossuaries with the bones of the deceased were placed.*

*(opposite) The* **Uzziah inscription** *on a stone tablet (14×13.6 inches [35×34 cm]) with the following text in Aramaic: "Hither were brought the bones of Uzziah, King of Judah. Do not open."*

*From this inscription we learn that the remains of King Uzziah were reinterred here in the Second Temple period, and this stone was used to seal off the burial niche. Although there is evidence that during the Second Temple period the tombs of the Davidic dynasty were left untouched* (Tosephta, Baba Batra *1, 7), it would seem that Uzziah was buried separately from the outset. The Bible asserts this in the verse: "and they buried him . . . in the field of the burial which belonged to the kings; for they said, He is a leper"* (2 *Chron. 26:23). Josephus states that he was "buried alone in his gardens"* (Antiquities *10, 227). Thus it would seem that it was possible to transfer Uzziah's remains from their original burial place.*

*The exact site where Uzziah was reinterred is unknown because the stone tablet was brought to the Russian Church on the Mount of Olives during the nineteenth century and placed among its antiquities collection without any reference to where it was found and how it was brought there. The tablet was identified in 1931 by Prof. E. L. Sukenik and in 1968 was purchased by the Israel Museum, where it is now on display.*

went numerous transformations, but no vestiges from the Second Temple period have been found. At its eastern boundary are the remnants of a broad wall, which in the opinion of scholars are remains of the Second Wall. However, they could be the vestiges of a broad wall that encompassed the pool itself.

Another pool dug during the Second Temple period was the Struthion Pool, which supplied water to the Antonia fortress and its vicinity. The pool was excavated near the northwestern corner of the Antonia, in the bed of the moat described above. It was a large open pool (approximately 171 × 46 feet [52 × 14 meters]), which collected the rainwater from the moat, and also apparently exploited the waters in the Hasmonean conduit, through which water from the upper section of the Tyropoeon Valley (the present-day Damascus Gate area) flowed into the cisterns on the Temple Mount. A pair of pools, which supplied the city in Herod's time, were called by explorers and Christian pilgrims the Bethesda Pools. They are identified with the Sheep's Pools (Probatica in Greek). Already in the Second Temple period these pools were apparently considered to have medicinal healing powers. At all events, during the Roman era a temple to the god of healing was erected.

Along the Beth Zetha Valley riverbed there was another pool—the Pool of Israel—which was formed during Herod's extension of the Temple Mount. A dam 46 feet (14 m) wide was erected to block up the riverbed. It was in this manner that the largest pool in Jerusalem was created. It was 328 feet (100 m) long, 125 feet (38 m) wide, and at its deepest point about 98 feet (30 m). In

*Reconstruction of a* **burial tomb** *or* **monument** *the remains of which were discovered by Conrad Schick in 1879, and reexcavated by Netzer and Ben-Arieh in the 1980s, about 820 feet (250 m) north of Damascus Gate. This was a circular structure, with two peripheral walls, one inside the other. The internal walls were built by the special* opus reticulatum *technique commonly used during Herod's reign. The external part was covered in cut stone in the style commonly used in other buildings of this period. Between the two walls was a vaulted roof, and the center of the building was covered with a conical roof. Similar burial tombs were found in Rome, such as those of the emperors Augustus and Hadrian, and elsewhere.*

*The site of this monument was within the Third Wall of Jerusalem, erected by Agrippa I. As burial tombs or monuments were generally placed outside the city walls, this particular structure can be dated to the period before the reign of Agrippa I. One theory has it that this structure is "Herod's Monument" mentioned by Josephus when describing the construction of the siege wall by Titus* (Wars 5, 3, 2; 5, 12, 2).

the 1930s, the Jerusalem municipality blocked it up, and a car park was built above it. Apart from the Siloam Pool, we have no definite information about other pools located in the Tyropoeon Valley, the city's central valley. However, there are signs which may be evidence of further pools, such as a broad dam across the Tyropoeon Valley underneath Wilson's Arch (it was the same width as the Pool of Israel dam—46 feet [14 m]). It would seem that this dam was also the beginning of a diversion canal which passed along the southwestern corner of the Temple Mount, below street level, in the direction of the Tyropoeon Valley toward the south.

Another pool that deserves mention is what is now called the Sultan's Pool, previously identified as the Serpent's Pool mentioned by Josephus (*Wars* 5, 3, 2). Trial trenches dug in it have not produced any evidence to confirm or refute the assumption that this pool existed during the Second Temple era. It seems that it was first used in the Byzantine period.

Water was also supplied to the city from springs south of Bethlehem through a system of aqueducts. The finds from the excavations in the Jewish Quarter and part of the conduit on Mount Zion have led to the conclusion that these spring waters were for the sole use of the Temple Mount. It would seem that these aqueducts were built in the Hasmonean era, at the end of the second century BCE, but were renovated over the years. The first time was apparently during Herod's rule and possibly again under the Roman governor Pontius Pilate. These aqueducts were also repaired a number of times in later eras and continued to function until the twentieth century.

Within the city itself, the use of cisterns built beneath the houses were common in Second Temple times. In the excavations in the Jewish Quarter, ritual baths, pools, and cisterns hewn out of the rock were discovered under many houses. These installations made it possible for the inhabitants to be independent of the natural spring—the Gihon Spring—and also made it possible for the city to expand in all directions. Cisterns were also dug on the Temple Mount, and already in the Letter of Aristeas water cisterns are mentioned as being present in the lower levels of the Temple Mount. We now have evidence of thirty-nine cisterns of various sizes. These cisterns were not all used for the supply of water during the Second Temple period. Three of

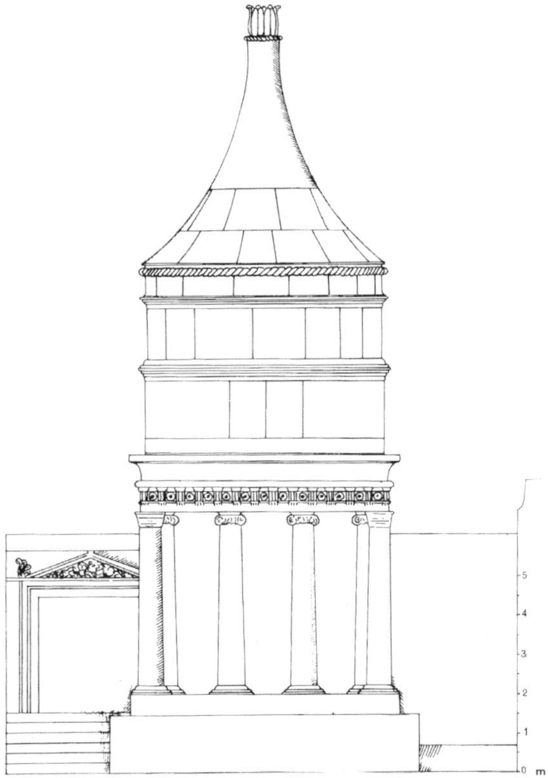


*The name of* **Absalom's Pillar** *originated in a Jewish tradition which considered that the monument in the Kidron Valley was that which Absalom, King David's son, erected to himself (2 Sam. 18:18). Since in Hebrew the word for monument and hand is the same, the usual drawings of the monument will show a hand at its apex. As Absalom revolted against his father, the Jews of Jerusalem used to throw stones at this monument, and wayward sons were also brought here to show them the fate of a rebellious son.*

*The structure, almost certainly built during Herod's reign, is hewn out of the rock, and thus stands apart from the surrounding rockface.*

*The structure is 26 feet (8 m) high. In its lower section is a burial chamber also hewn out of the rock. This is a square chamber with room for two bodies.*

*Above the burial chamber is the circular roof built of finely cut stone. Above that is a conical structure made out of a single stone, and at its apex a calyx decorated in the shape of a flower bud.*

*The burial chamber was broken open in the Byzantine era, and was used by monks as living quarters, as in many of the burial caves in the Kidron Valley.*

*In 2000, a Christian inscription, with the name of James, the brother of Jesus, was discovered on the monument.*

The **Tomb of the Kings** *is the name by which the large burial cave is known. It is one of the most beautiful of its type in Jerusalem and it is situated some 2,625 feet (800 m) north of the Old City wall. (The illustration shows the reconstruction of the facade of the tomb.)*

*According to one tradition, the kings of the Davidic dynasty were buried here. Another tradition claims that it belonged to Calba Savua, the father-in-law of Rabbi Akiva. Today most scholars agree that probably Queen Helene and members of the Adiabene royal family were buried here in the first century* CE. *The theory that the tomb was the burial place of royalty is supported by the fact that one of the sarcophagi found here bore the Aramaic inscription "Queen Ṣaddan."*

*Josephus* (Antiquities *20, 4, 3) states that the burial cave was embellished with three most impressive pyramids. Even today the magnificence of the burial cave's facade is apparent—it is decorated with a frieze, and the frame of the entrance is embossed with engravings of clusters of grapes, acanthus leaves, fruit and flower wreaths. The cave entrance was closed off with a burial stone which is still* in situ *nearby. It was moved by a secret mechanism, evidence of which was found inside the cave.*

*Some of the sarcophagi found inside the cave were taken to the Louvre Museum in Paris, while others were placed in various building projects on the Temple Mount when renovations were carried out during the 1860s. They were all elaborately decorated in Hellenistic style.*

them served as entrances to the Temple Mount, for example, Warren's Gate (cistern no. 30) and Barclay's Gate (cistern 19). The system of water cisterns, which developed in the Second Temple period, was used in Jerusalem until the mid-twentieth century, and throughout the centuries served as the main source of water for the city's inhabitants. The water for these cisterns was conducted through aqueducts from Solomon's Pools and from the vicinity of the Damascus Gate (by way of the Struthion Pool). Other cisterns were filled with rainwater.

To complete the picture of Jerusalem in the Second Temple period we must also mention its cemeteries. The pattern of the city's burial grounds is in the main well known to us, since the graves situated around it were not affected by the wars which it endured (they were ruined mainly as the result of building activities beginning from the end of the nineteenth century). In Jerusalem an amazing dispersion of graves was found surrounding the Old City itself, in localities which were outside its boundaries during the various stages of its development during the Second Temple period. The majority of the graves are groups of family burial caves hewn out of the relatively soft rock.

*A* **decoration** *typical of Second Temple period Jewish art found on one of the most splendid sarcophagi from that period. The sarcophagus was discovered in the burial tomb perhaps belonging to Herod's family, which was outstanding in its magnificence. (The sarcophagus is now on display in the Greek Patriarchate Museum in Jerusalem.) Herod's family tomb is mentioned by Josephus in his account of the siege of Jerusalem by Titus in 70* CE (Wars 3, 2), *and this has led to its being identified with the burial cave found in the vicinity of the King David Hotel.*

*The* **Tomb of Zechariah** *and the* **Tomb of Hezir's Priestly Family** *(cross section below) are two of the most well-known burial caves in the Kidron Valley, situated opposite the southeastern corner of the Temple Mount. (The third, Absalom's Pillar, to the left of these tombs, is not included in this diagram.)*

*The tomb of Hezir's priestly family, from the middle of the first century* BCE *(the beginning of Roman rule), is the burial cave of a family of priests known from the historical sources. An inscription on the tomb reads: "This is (the) tomb and the monument of El'azar, Hanniah, Yo'ezer, Judah, Simon, Johanan, the sons of Joseph, son of Oved. Joseph and El'azar sons of Hanniah—priests of the Hezir family. The word* nefesh *(here translated as "monument") is literally "spirit," and it is possible that the tombstone was placed to the left of the entrance with the columns. There are intimations of a structure—perhaps a pyramid—as was customary at the time in graves hewn out of the rock or built up within it.*

*Prior to the discovery of the inscription, Jewish tradition considered this tomb to be the "house set apart" (Beth Hahofshit), the place where King Uzziah dwelt after he was smitten with leprosy and expelled from Jerusalem (2 Chron. 26:21). The inscription confirms that this was the tomb of the Hezir family, while the names of the other two tombs are based on tradition only.*

*The tomb of Zechariah was apparently built at the beginning of the first century* CE, *but it is not known for whom it was intended. It appears that its construction was not completed and therefore may never have been used for burial. To the right of the Tomb of Zechariah is another rock-hewn tomb. In view of the evidence in the "Copper Scroll" (one of the Dead Sea Scrolls), this tomb may be identified as belonging to the priest Zadok.*

**The Siege of Titus, 70 CE**
Map legend:

- Jews
- Romans
- Positioning of Roman forces
- Roman camp
- Battlesite
- Retreat
- Roman siege ramp
- Siege wall
- Area burned by the Romans
- (5, 3, 1) Passage from *The Jewish War*

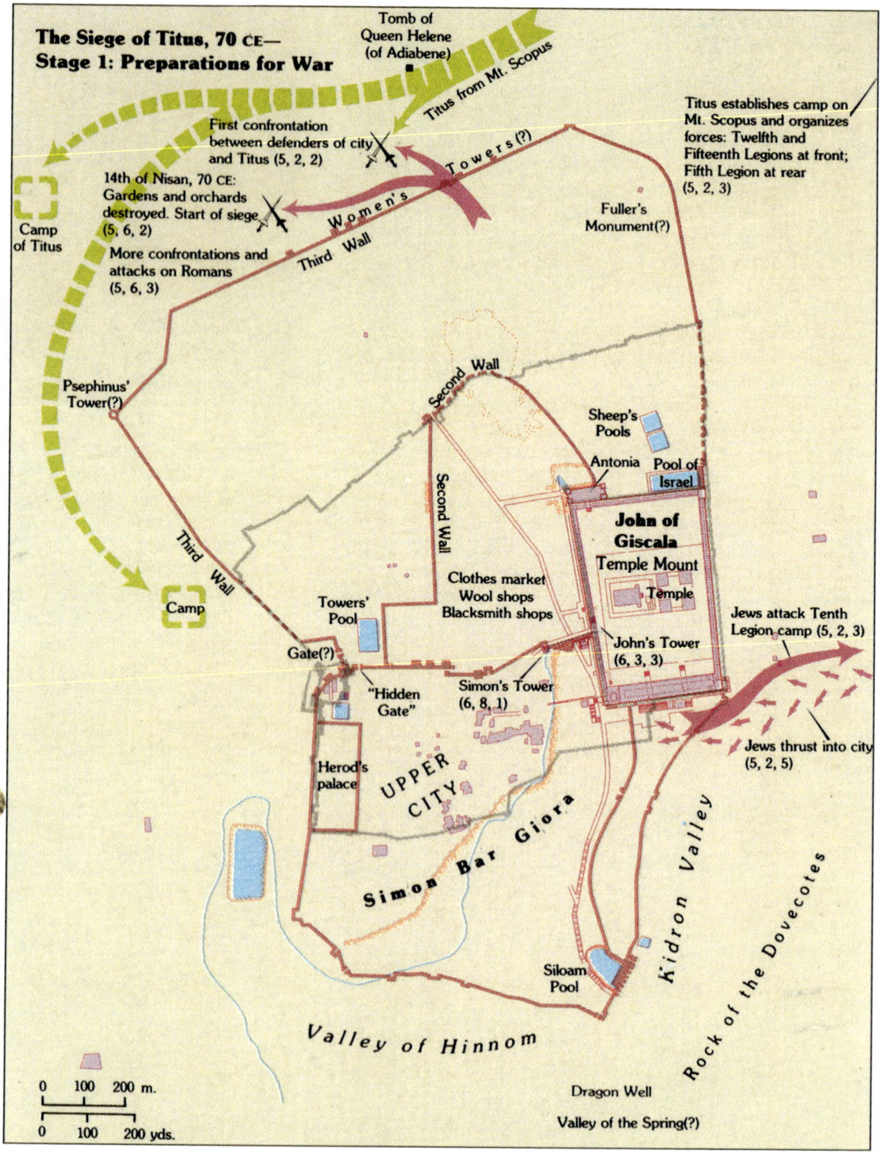

*An engraving of a* **menorah** *(candelabrum), with a triangular base, 8 inches (20 cm) high, found only a few hundred feet from the site where the Temple menorah stood. Additional engravings were discovered at the site depicting what seems to be the altar and the table of the shewbread. This engraving of the menorah, as well as that on a coin from the reign of Matthias Antigonus, and to a certain extent the menorah on the Arch of Titus in Rome, are the only illustrations extant of the original menorah in the Temple, and were engraved when it was still in use there.*

*The engraving was made on plaster, apparently at the time of Herod. It was found together with a Herodian coin beneath the floor of a building from the Herodian period, or that of one of his descendants. This was not the original site and thus it can be assumed that the building on whose wall the menorah was engraved was demolished during Herod's reign, or shortly after his death.*

## The Siege of Titus, 70 CE—Stage 2: Capture of the Second and Third Walls

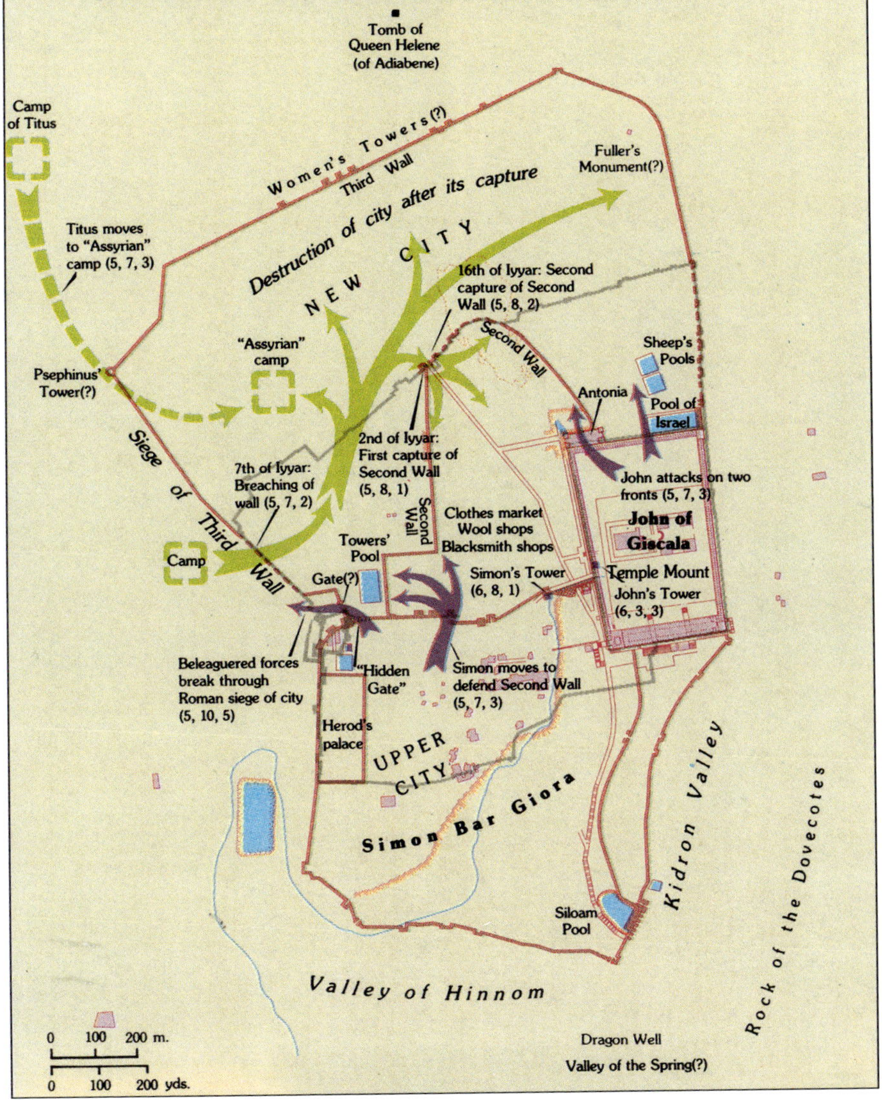

**Judaea Capta** *engraved on a gold coin minted in Rome in honor of the Roman victory over Judaea. On the face of the coin is the bust of the Roman emperor Vespasian, and on its obverse is "Judaea" sitting in mourning beside a plundered statue, underneath which is the Latin inscription "Judaea," for Judaea Capta.*

*The* **sewage channel**. *In the Second Temple period a city street ran northward from the Siloam Pool up along the Western Wall. The street is beautifully paved with stone-dressed margins, typical of the Herodian period.*

*Under the street's pavement, a well-made sewage channel, lined with large stones, was installed. The lowest section of the channel's course was diverted west of the street in order not to pollute the Siloam Pool.*

*According to Josephus Flavius, during the Roman siege of Jerusalem, and after parts of the city were conquered, many of the inhabitants found refuge in these channels, only later to be hunted by the Roman troops.*

**The Siege of Titus, 70 CE—Stage 3: Capture of the Antonia and Breach of the Temple Mount**

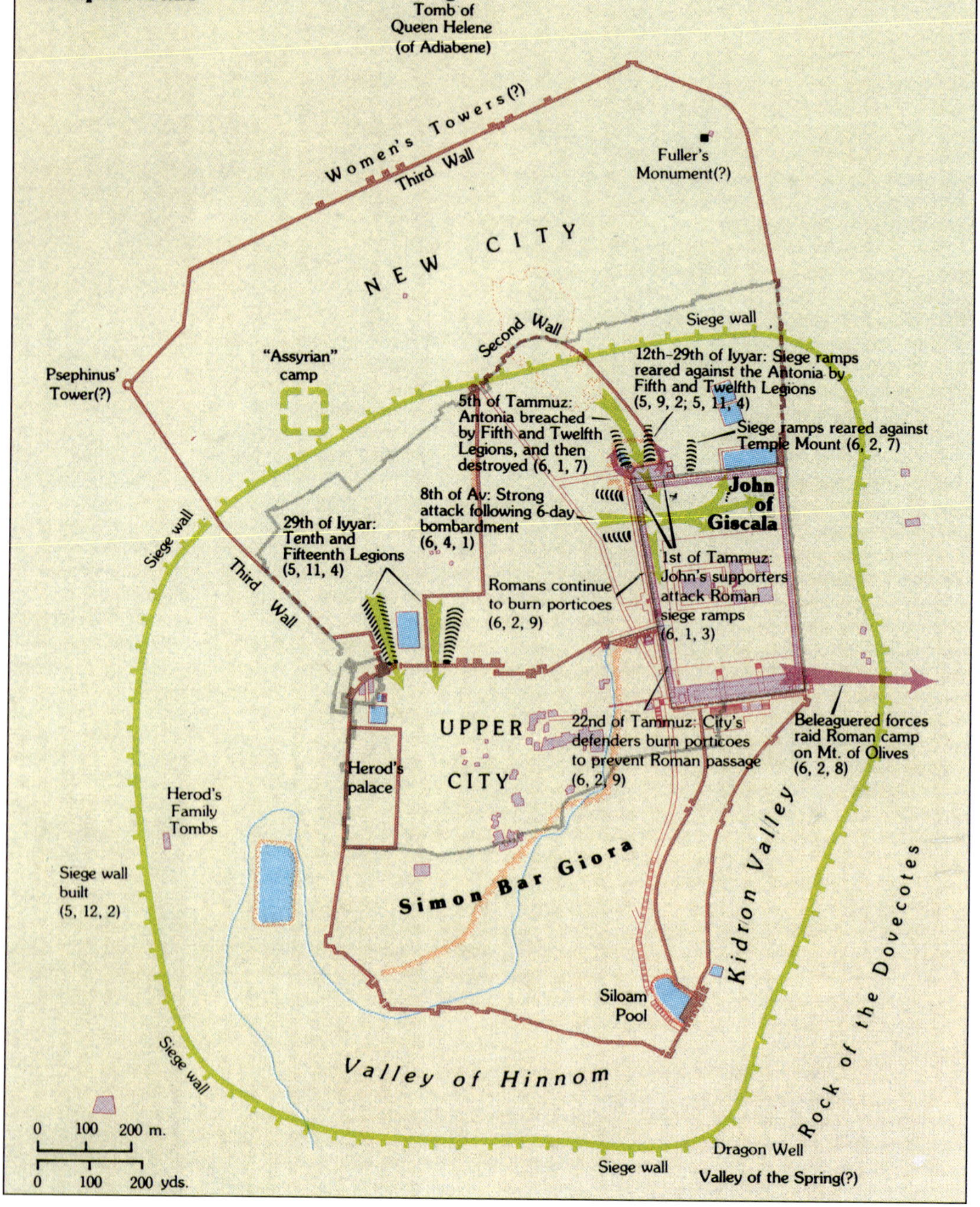

## The Siege of Titus, 70 CE—Stage 4: Capture of the Temple Mount, Upper City, and Lower City

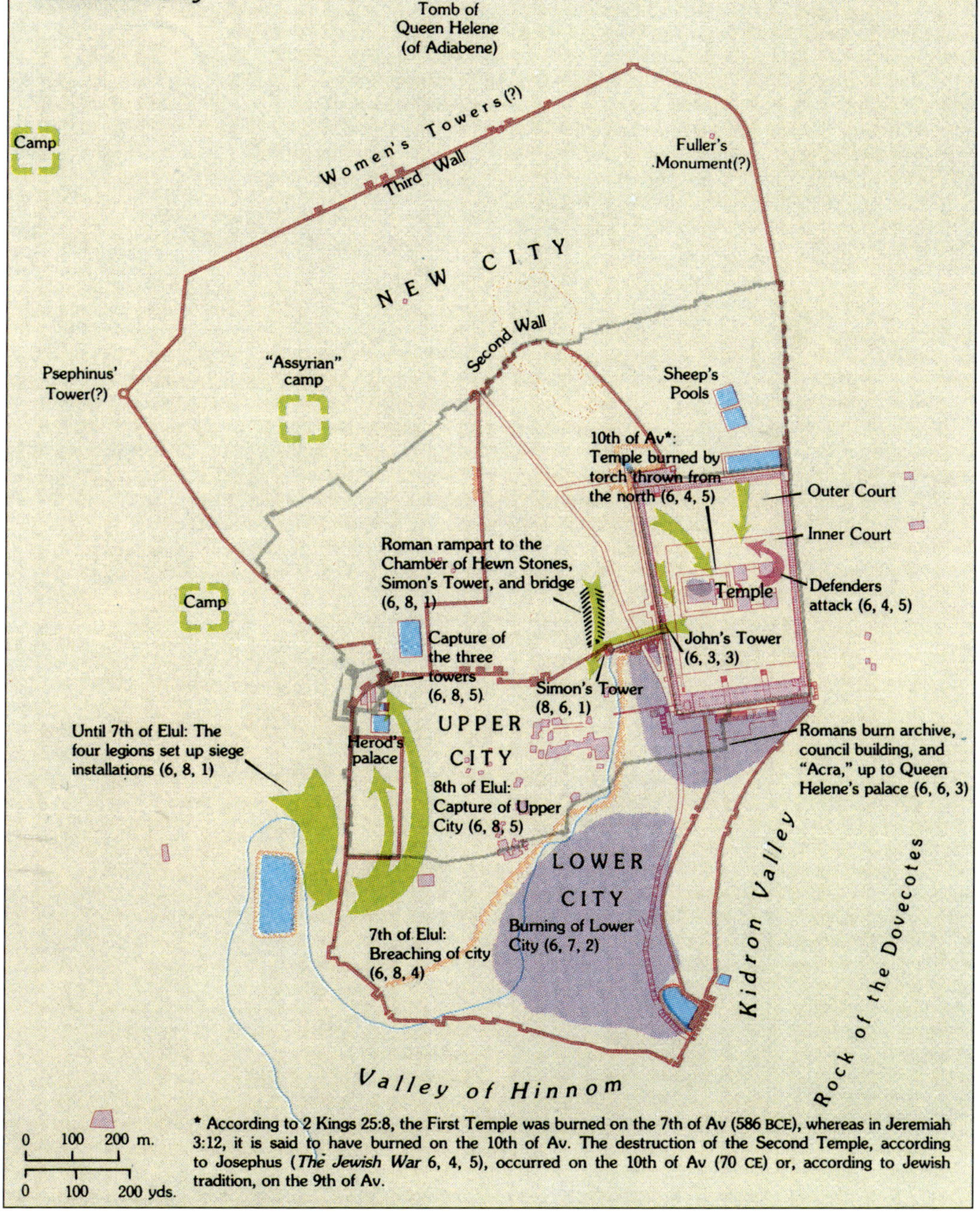


* According to 2 Kings 25:8, the First Temple was burned on the 7th of Av (586 BCE), whereas in Jeremiah 3:12, it is said to have burned on the 10th of Av. The destruction of the Second Temple, according to Josephus (*The Jewish War* 6, 4, 5), occurred on the 10th of Av (70 CE) or, according to Jewish tradition, on the 9th of Av.

# Jerusalem at the Time of Jesus

In the beginning of the Common Era, Jerusalem generally appeared as is shown in the previous chapter during the time of Herod the Great. The king's great works—the rebuilding of the Temple and its artificial mount, the Second Wall, and all the other public buildings which he added to the city—were already in existence and serve as background to the evangelical narrative of the Gospels.

Parts of the city, as shown on the map of Jerusalem at the end of the Second Temple period, were added after the death of Jesus. These include the Third Wall, and the neighborhood of Bezetha included within it.

Although the New Testament serves as an important source for the study of Jerusalem in the time of Jesus, it is sparing in descriptive details of the city. We must therefore base our knowledge on the descriptions of Josephus Flavius and of the Mishnah, as is the case when studying Jerusalem in the year 70 CE. Usually, the New Testament mentions only the name of a place without any distinguishing feature which would help us to identify it today.

When relating to the Christian traditions surrounding the holy sites in the city, one should bear in mind that the Christian community which remained in the city after its destruction in 70 CE was small and poor. Furthermore, although no documentation remains concerning the sites that were considered holy, or about their precise location, they were most likely on Mount Zion. Moreover, when Jerusalem became a pagan city in 135 CE, the persecution of Christians by the Roman authorities precluded the development and maintenance of the holy places, and thus, many of the authentic sites simply disappeared, leaving no traces. However, the discovery of an ancient drawing of a Christian pilgrim in the Church of the Holy Sepulcher indicates that the site was venerated by Christians in the second century.

In the fourth century, when Christianity be-

**Map** *drawn in 1580 by* **Heinrich Bünting** *(1545–1606), a native of Hanover (whose emblem consists of clover leaves). Although a late map, it stresses the popular perception of Jerusalem as the center of the world and its significance in the life of Jesus. Its function as the pivot of three continents reflects Jerusalem's central role in world events arising out of Christ's connection with it.*

*America, known at the time for only about one hundred years, is here called Terra Nova, and appears in the lower left-hand corner of the map.*

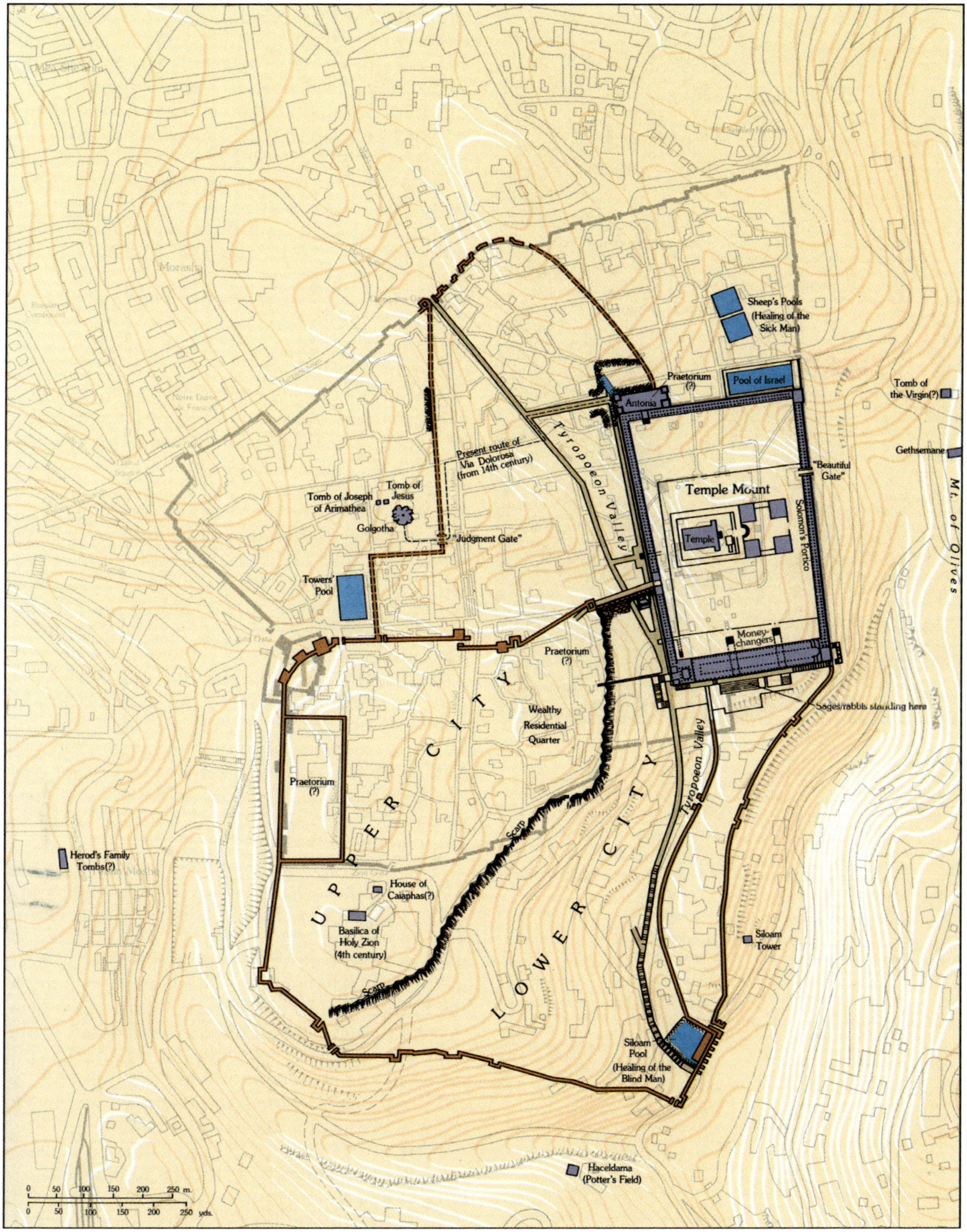
Sheep's Pools (Healing of the Sick Man)
Praetorium (?)
Pool of Israel
Antonia
Tomb of the Virgin(?)
Gethsemane
Mt. of Olives
"Beautiful Gate"
Temple Mount
Temple
Solomon's Portico
Tyropoeon Valley
Present route of Via Dolorosa (from 14th century)
Tomb of Joseph of Arimathea
Tomb of Jesus
Golgotha
"Judgment Gate"
Towers' Pool
Praetorium (?)
Money-changers
Sages/rabbis standing here
Wealthy Residential Quarter
UPPER CITY
LOWER CITY
Tyropoeon Valley
Praetorium (?)
Herod's Family Tombs(?)
House of Caiaphas(?)
Basilica of Holy Zion (4th century)
Scarp
Scarp
Siloam Tower
Siloam Pool (Healing of the Blind Man)
Haceldama (Potter's Field)
0 50 100 150 200 250 m.
0 50 100 150 200 250 yds.

**David's Tower**, *with the exception of the Temple Mount, is the most impressive of the remains of Second Temple period Jerusalem. In the time of Jesus, it was named the Hippicus Tower, built by Herod the Great to commemorate a friend of his by this name. Nevertheless, David's dynasty, to which Jesus is ascribed, left its profound impression on the Christians of the city. The connection between King David and his city led to the renaming of the tower already by the early community of Christians in the city, while the gate to the west of the tower had also borne the name of King David.*

*For the Christians, David's Tower symbolizes the "earthly" Jerusalem and during the Crusader period—when Jerusalem received its utmost expression as both the Earthly and the Heavenly City—David's Tower, as well as the Church of the Holy Sepulcher and the Dome of the Rock, became the most important symbols of Jerusalem.*

*Today, erroneously, the name "David's Tower" refers to the seventeenth minaret of the Citadel.*

came the dominant religion and could be observed openly, the Christians built churches at various points in the city they believed to be the true sites of the evangelical events. The fact that the identification of the holy places in the first Christian period (the Byzantine period) was refuted in the second Christian period (the Crusader period), reflects the difficulties in authenticating the holy sites. The three centuries of obscurity, from the first to the fourth century CE, contributed to the dubiousness regarding the actual sites where the events occurred.

In addition, even to the present day, the Eastern and Western churches, as well as the various denominations, have conflicting traditions, adding to the difficulties.

The only holy site which has been thoroughly excavated and studied is the Church of the Holy Sepulcher, the traditional site of Jesus' crucifixion, burial, and resurrection. The result of the study can be summarized as follows.

During the First and Second Temple periods, the site served as a quarry, a place suitable for both executions and burials. Proof of this is provided by the numerous burial caves discovered within the premises of the church and the immediate vicinity. Moreover, the descriptions of the fourth-century church fathers concerning the works carried out at the site, first by Hadrian and then by Constantine the Great, indicate the difficulties faced by builders at this quarry. In addition, the existence of contemporary burial caves at the site is a good indication that at that time the church was located outside the city wall (that is, the Second Wall). This, therefore, adds to the authenticity of the Holy Sepulcher.

Naturally, one would expect to have the same simple explanation for the Via Dolorosa, which plays such an important role in the minds of millions of believers. However, the whole concept of the Via Dolorosa, as it is perceived today, began in the Crusader period, when on Palm Sunday the faithful would pass through the Golden Gate onto the Temple Mount, thereby imitating the triumphal entry of Jesus into Jerusalem. The pilgrims would then continue to the Church of the Holy Sepulcher through the "Gates of Sorrow" in the western wall of the Temple Mount.

This is the origin of the route of the Via Dolorosa. Its final course—as it runs today—was ascribed only in the fourteenth century. This was due to the prohibition of entry to the Temple

Mount by Christians, who thus sought a route aligned outside it. The Stations of the Cross have not been included in the map because, although the Via Dolorosa clearly ends in the Church of the Holy Sepulcher, its initial point remains obscure.

This starting point, according to the Gospels, is the site where Pontius Pilate condemned Jesus to death. The sources make no reference to the location of the site (the Praetorium). Only in John 19:13 is there a more detailed description. Even this account, however, is not sufficiently specific, and three possible locations have been considered.

The first is the Antonia fortress at the northwestern corner of the Temple Mount. This has been the traditional site for the Praetorium ever since Crusader times, but in the Byzantine period, and for a long time thereafter, a certain church (St. Sophia), which must have stood somewhere near today's Western Wall plaza, was thought to have commemorated the event.

This leads us to a second possibility: Pontius Pilate used the Hasmonean palace (located in the present-day Jewish Quarter) as his residence, making this the site where the trial of Jesus took place. However, other scholars suggest he would have preferred the luxurious palace of King Herod, near the present-day Citadel. Acceptance

*The* **Sheep's Pools** *were built in the Beth Zetha Valley which began at the present-day American Colony, passed through the Old City wall near the Rockefeller Museum and ended in the Kidron Valley in the vicinity of the Lions' Gate. A number of dams and some of the largest pools in Jerusalem such as the Pool of Israel were constructed in this valley. As the archaeological evidence has shown, the northern pool was first dug at the end of the First Temple period, and the other pool was added in the Hellenistic era at the beginning of the second century* BCE*, apparently at the initiative of the High Priest Simon. It continued to exist, as depicted here, until the destruction of the Second Temple.*

*The reconstruction of the pools is based mainly on Christian sources. These pools were held to be holy because of the miracle attributed to Jesus at their edge, and the porticoes surrounding them are described in detail in the New Testament. It is generally believed that sheep were washed here before being offered up as sacrifice in the Temple, hence the name Sheep's Pools.*

of any one of these theories would necessitate a change in the course of the Via Dolorosa.

A site that had an important role in both early and modern Christianity is the Basilica of Holy Zion, which served as an assembly place for the early Christian community in Jerusalem. Its long history has yet to be studied, but for pilgrims who come to Jerusalem, the Basilica of Holy Zion is second in importance only to that of the Holy Sepulcher. Remains of this fourth-century basilica were discovered.

But again there is a gap between the first-century residential quarter discovered on the site and the fourth-century Byzantine church, remains of which have been uncovered in a considerably well-preserved state. Very little is really known of events that occurred between the first and fourth centuries.

Other sites in Jerusalem mentioned in the Gospels include Gethsemane (Matt. 26:36–46, Mark 14:32), Haceldama (Matt. 27:6–8), the Siloam Pool (John 9:1–12), and Solomon's Portico (John 10:23; Acts 3:11, 5:12). All these sites are of great significance, as they provide information concerning not only the topography of the Holy Land, but also the customs and lifestyle of the communities that inhabited the city at the time of Jesus.

Although there is no doubt about the existence of the sites during this period, our knowledge is still lacking as a result of the three missing centuries of information.

*A* **mounting stone** *dating to the Crusader period, installed in the Church of Bethany, the site where Jesus began his triumphal entry into the Holy City. The stone depicts this scene (shown here) and others from the life of Christ, such as the resurrection of Lazarus.*

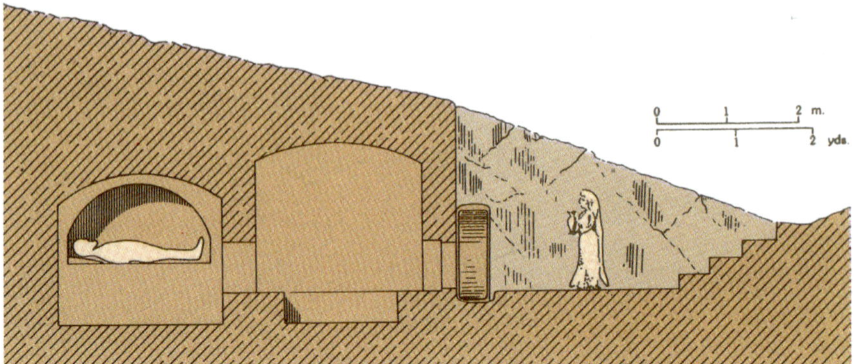


*A 1922 reconstruction of* **Jesus' tomb**. *This is a typical burial cave with a rolling stone at its opening. The form of bedrock as shown is based on conjecture, as it is known that the area served as a quarry. Generations of pilgrims chipped away pieces of the rock as souvenirs, thus completely distorting the shape of the tombs.*

# Index

Page numbers in italics refer to maps and illustrations or their captions.